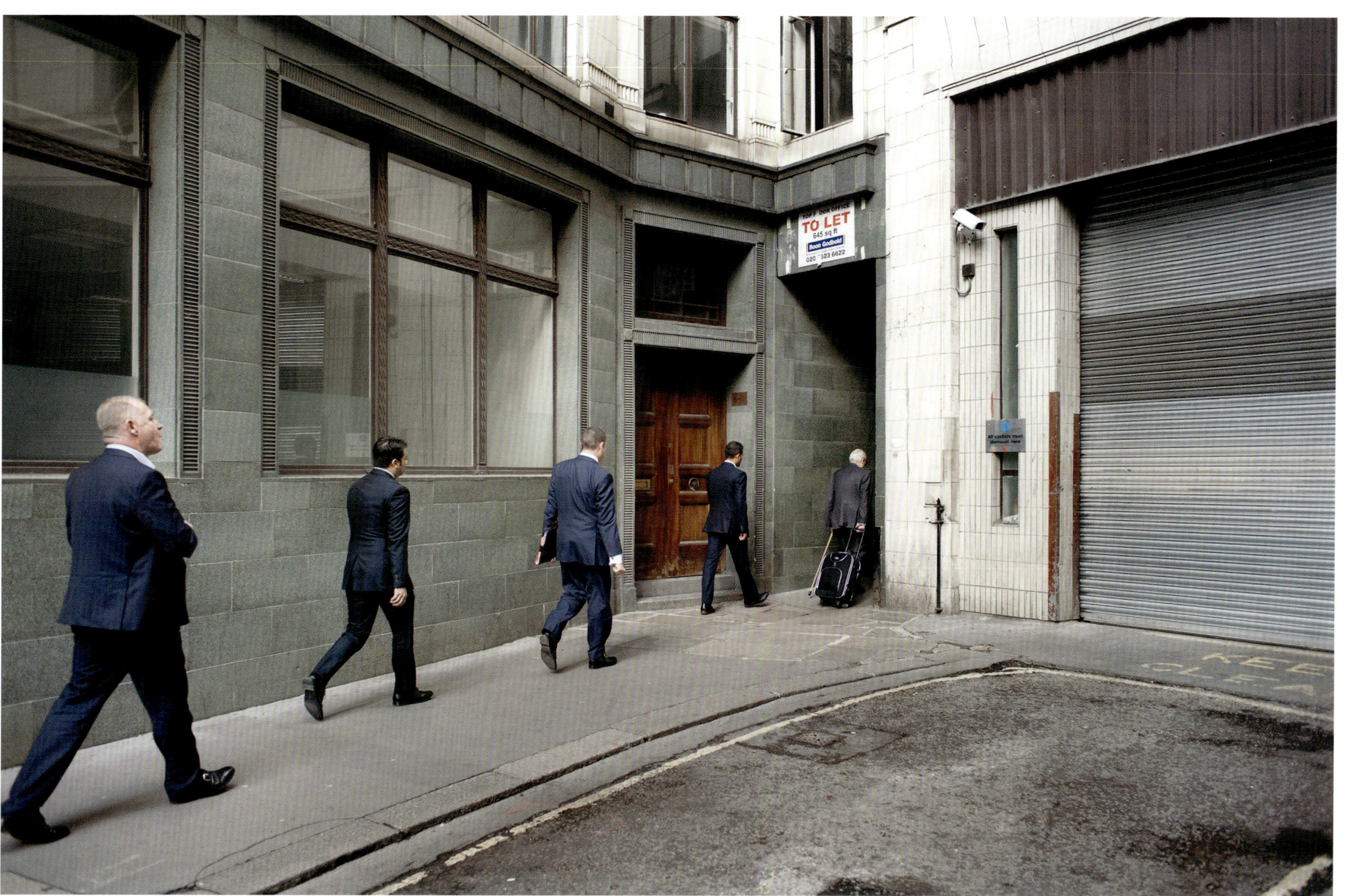
TO LET
645 sq ft
Boon Godbold

Publisher: Michael Itkoff
Creative Director: Ursula Damm
Copy Editor: Gabrielle Fastman

ISBN: 978-1-954119-51-2

Printed by Ofset Yapimevi, Turkey

Daylight Books
E-mail: info@daylightbooks.org
Web: www.daylightbooks.org

Daylight

CIPHER CITY

StreetMax

For Kate

PLAYING THE TRADITIONS: *CIPHER CITY* BY STREETMAX

by Zsolt Bátori

At first encounter, the photographs of StreetMax may seem puzzling to the unsuspecting viewer. They appear straightforward enough, but they resist quick comprehension. One quickly realizes that they demand more time, attention, and mental effort than most photographs, even within the realm of fine-art photography. This difficulty, however, is not a flaw but a strength. The challenge arises because StreetMax's photographs are remarkably complex and multilayered in their meaning, requiring viewers to engage in a process of discovery.

A casual glance at his work often leads to a striking first impression: the images seem staged. The people who populate his street photographs appear distributed with such precision and rhythm that one could easily believe they had been carefully arranged. The visual balance and order in these pictures seem too deliberate to have been left to chance. It is therefore understandable that many initially conclude that StreetMax is a director who orchestrates his scenes rather than a street photographer who simply observes them.

Yet this initial assumption is mistaken. StreetMax is not a director but a patient and perceptive observer. His photographs are not the result of staging but of waiting—waiting for the world to present itself in constellations so unique and ephemeral that they warrant preservation as images. In this sense, his practice aligns with the strictest traditions of street photography, where the task of the photographer is not to manipulate or construct reality but to recognize and capture fleeting moments of order, beauty, or significance within it. The apparent staging is, in fact, a product of his discipline and timing, not his intervention.

This distinction places StreetMax squarely within the lineage of straight photography, a tradition that emerged in the early twentieth century with the demand that photographers engage directly with the world as it is. Straight photographers rejected artificial manipulation and insisted that true artistry lay in discerning the photographic potential of reality itself. StreetMax adheres to this principle with remarkable rigor. His images testify to the possibility of finding rhythm, geometry, and coherence in everyday urban life without resorting to fabrication.

What makes his work particularly compelling is the tension it creates between appearance and reality. The viewer's first impression—that these must be staged photographs—must be overcome through reflection and deeper looking. In this way, StreetMax's art actively engages the audience in a process of discovery. His images challenge our assumptions about what we see, how we interpret photographic evidence, and where we locate the boundary between artifice and observation. They ask us to recognize how perception itself can be deceiving, and how photography, as both an art form and a cultural practice, mediates between truth and illusion.

In the end, the photographs of StreetMax remind us that tradition is not merely something to be repeated but something to be played with, questioned, and reinterpreted. By working within the conventions of straight and street photography while simultaneously unsettling our expectations of them, he breathes new life into these venerable genres. His art demands not just passive viewing but active engagement, rewarding those willing to pause, reconsider, and discover anew what lies within the frame.

Cipher City must be deciphered.

Zsolt Bátori is a philosopher of art, photography theorist, photographer, and curator. He holds a PhD in philosophy from Rutgers University and has taught and conducted research at universities in Hungary, the United States, Spain, and Argentina. His photographic work has been exhibited internationally. He is the founding director and curator of PH21 Gallery Barcelona and has served as a juror for Photolucida Critical Mass since 2023.

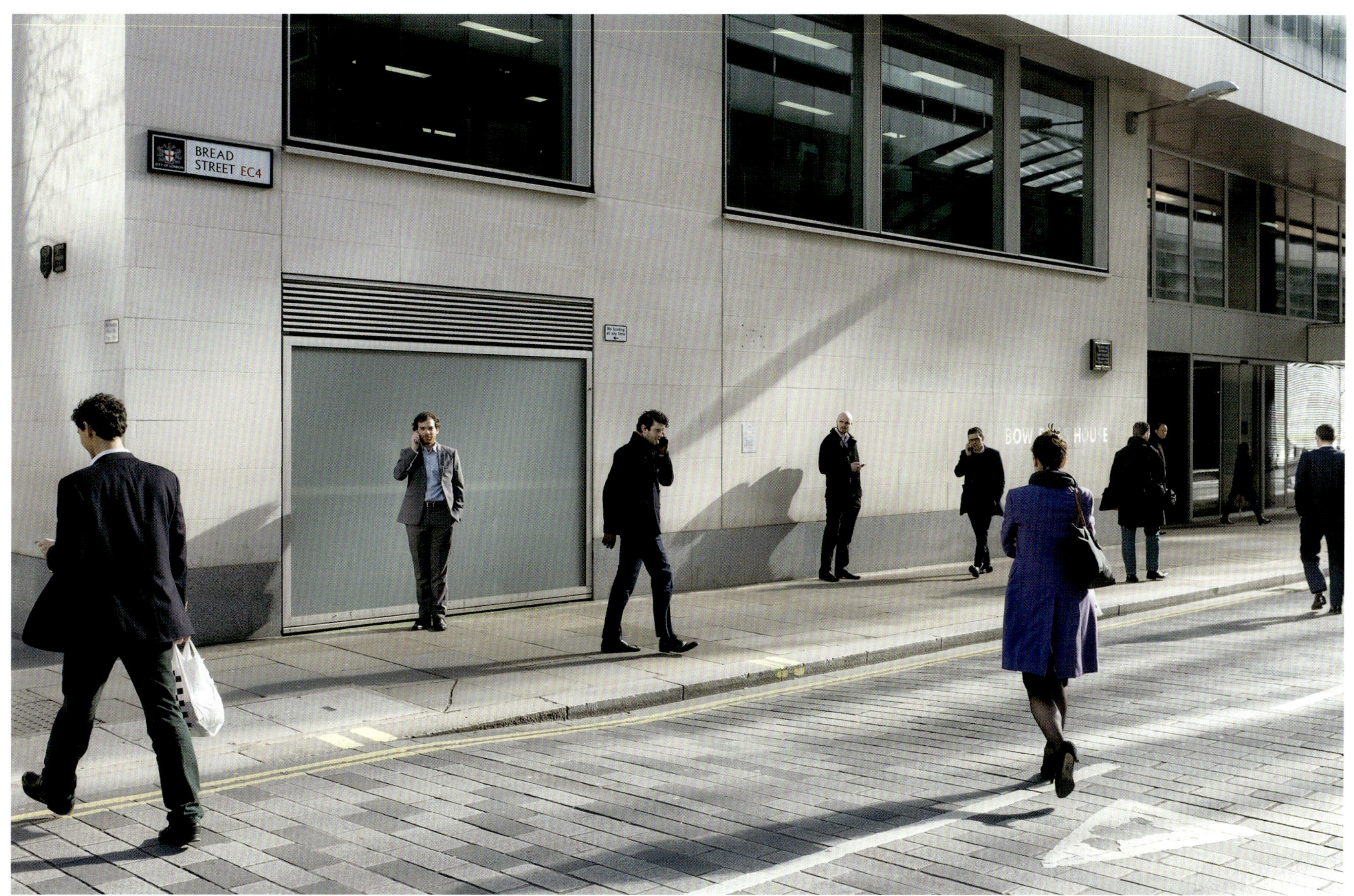
BREAD
STREET EC4

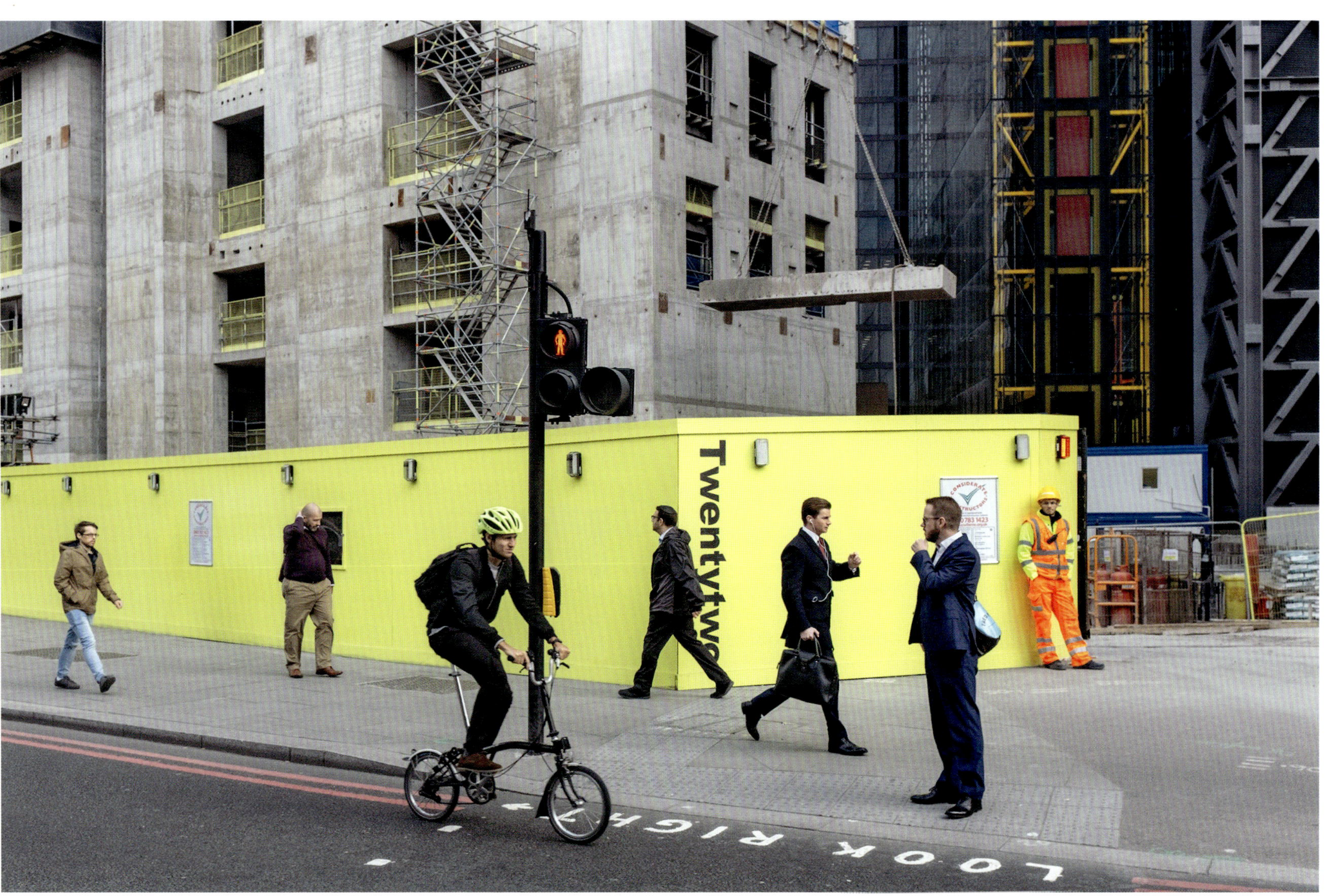
Twentytw
LOOK RIGHT

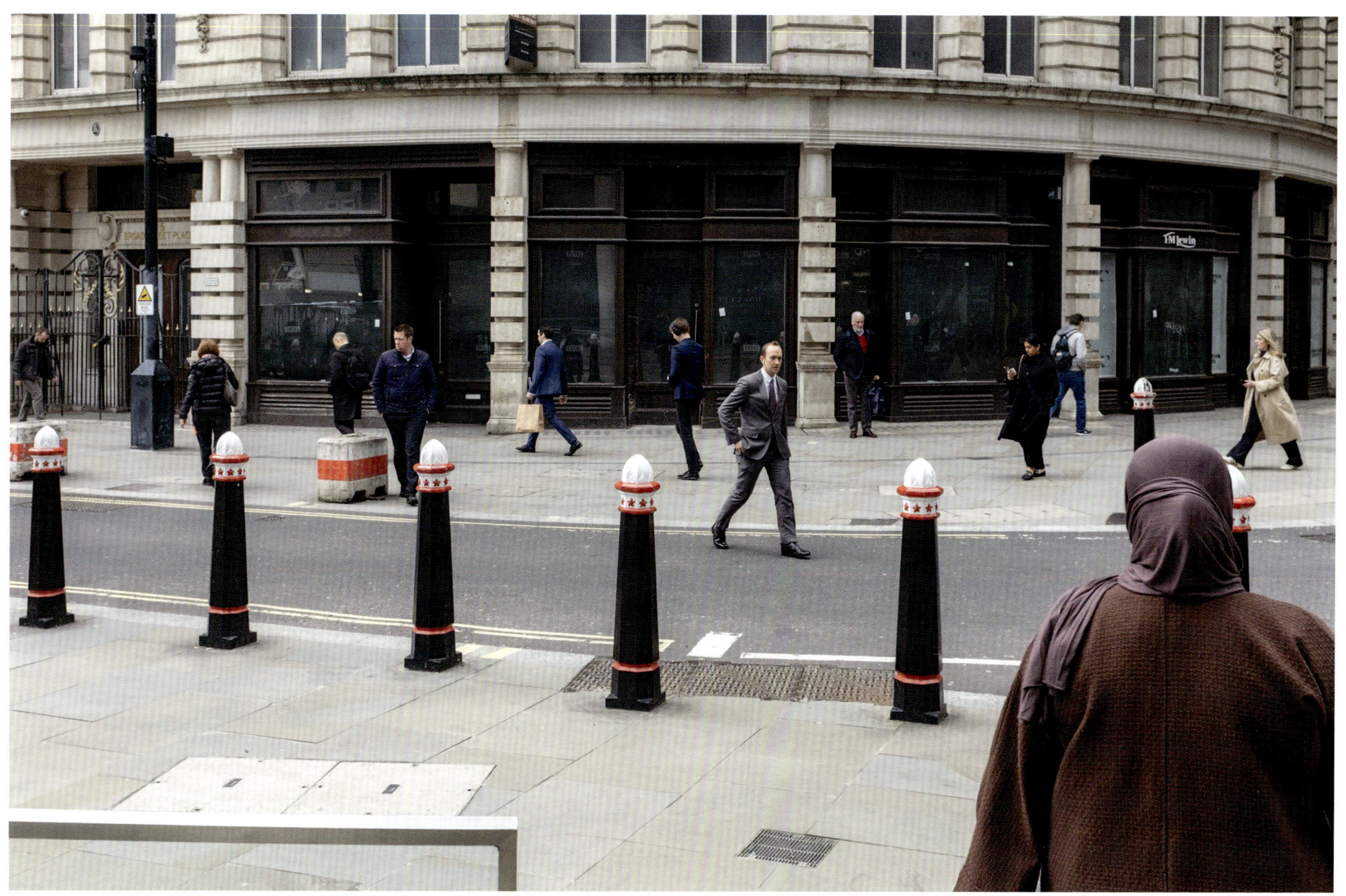
TM Lewin

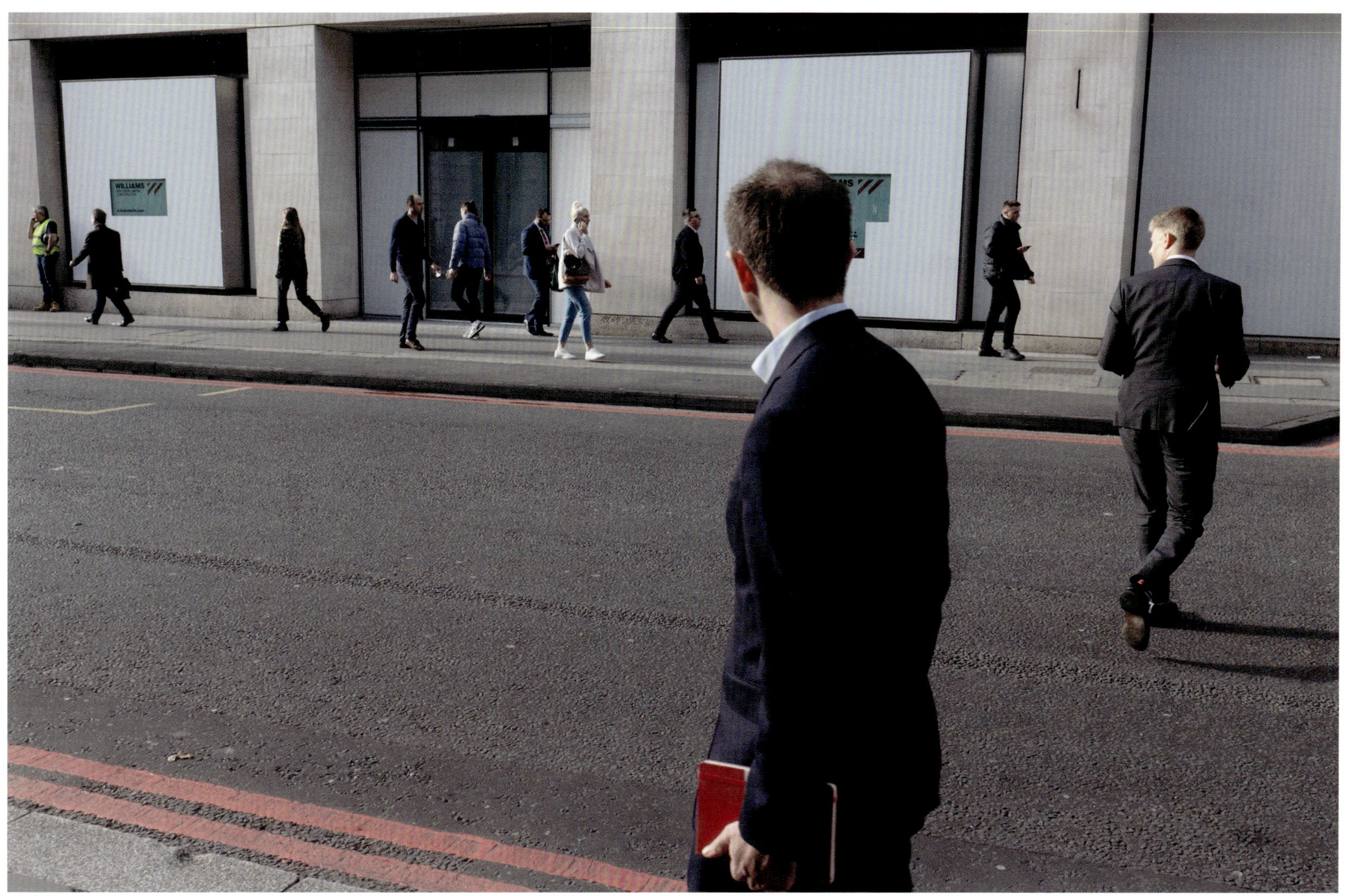
WILLIAMS

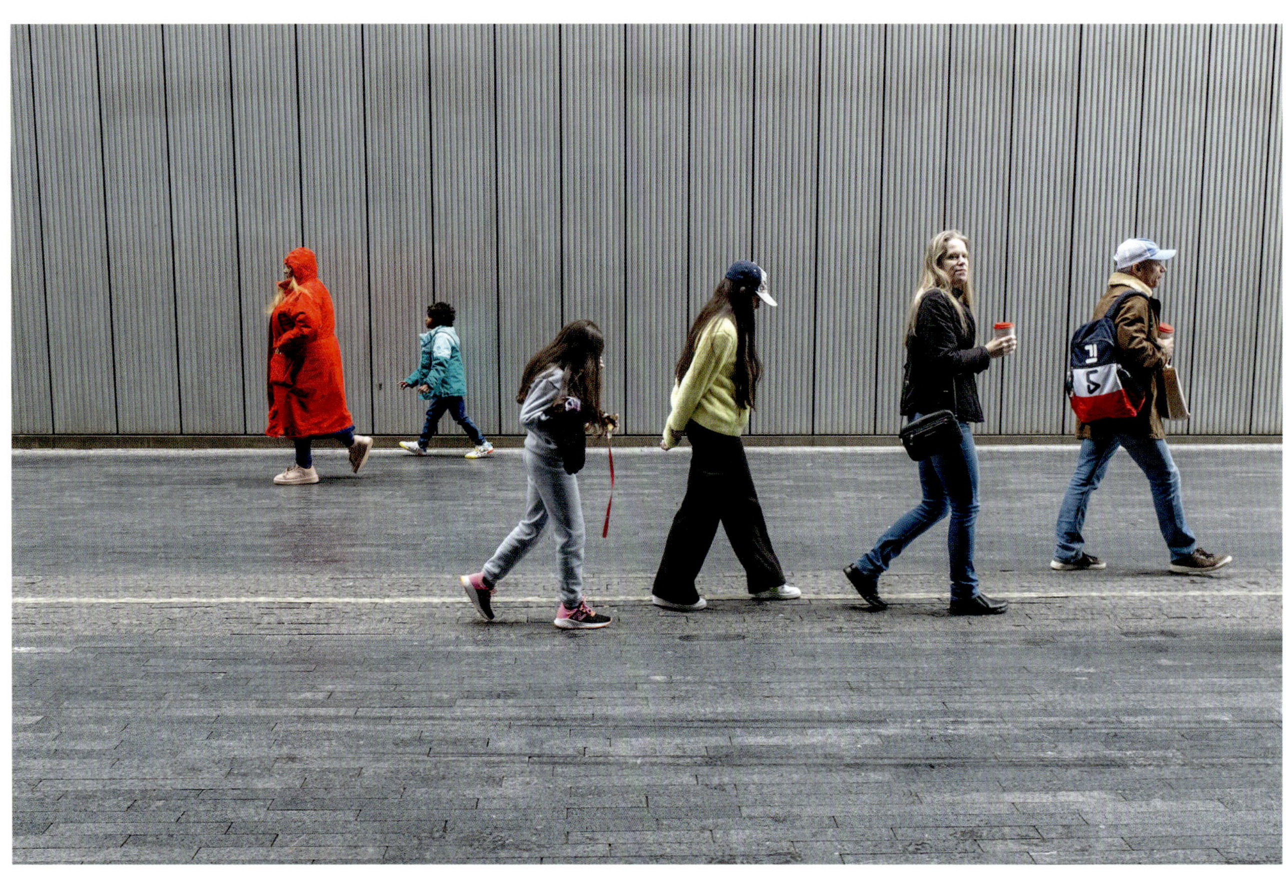

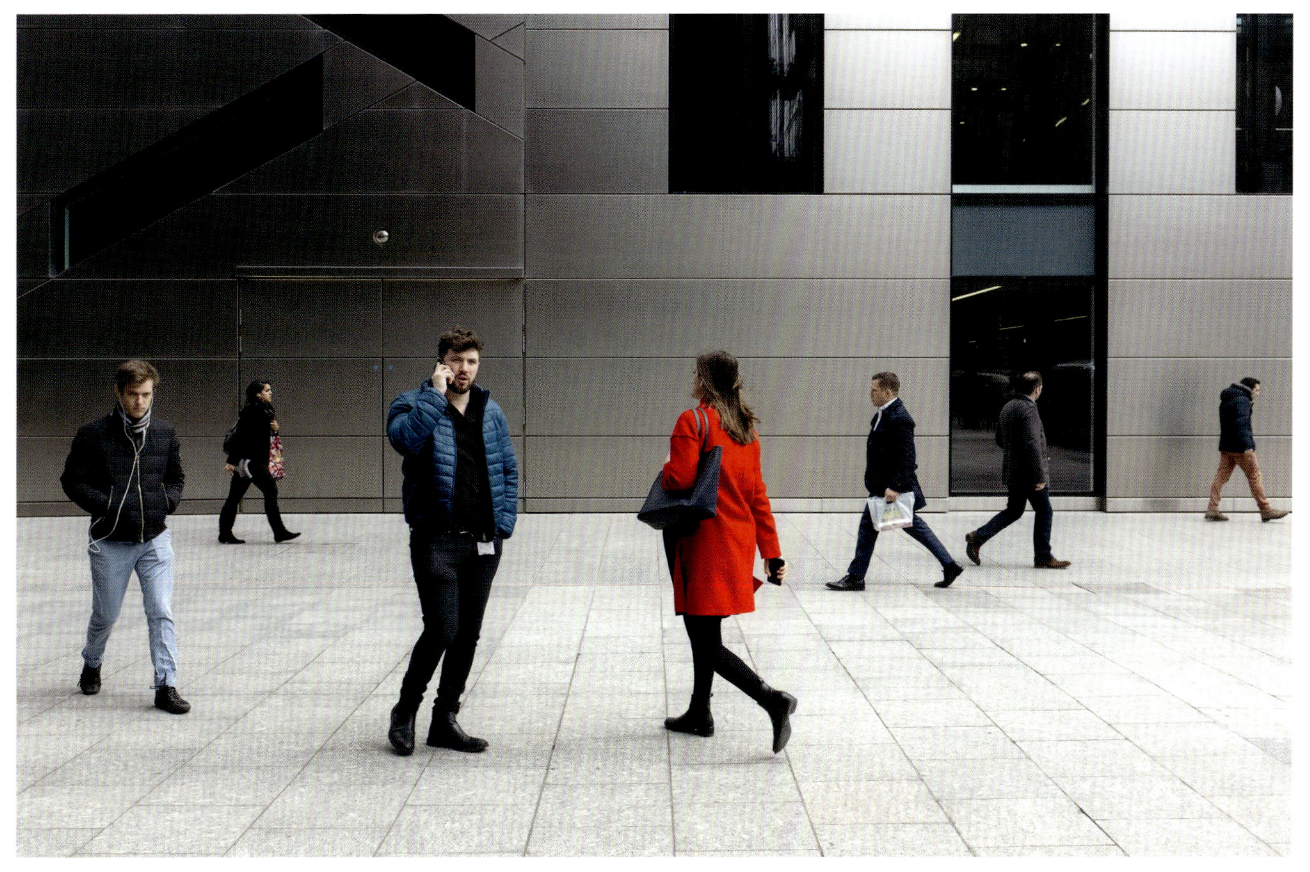

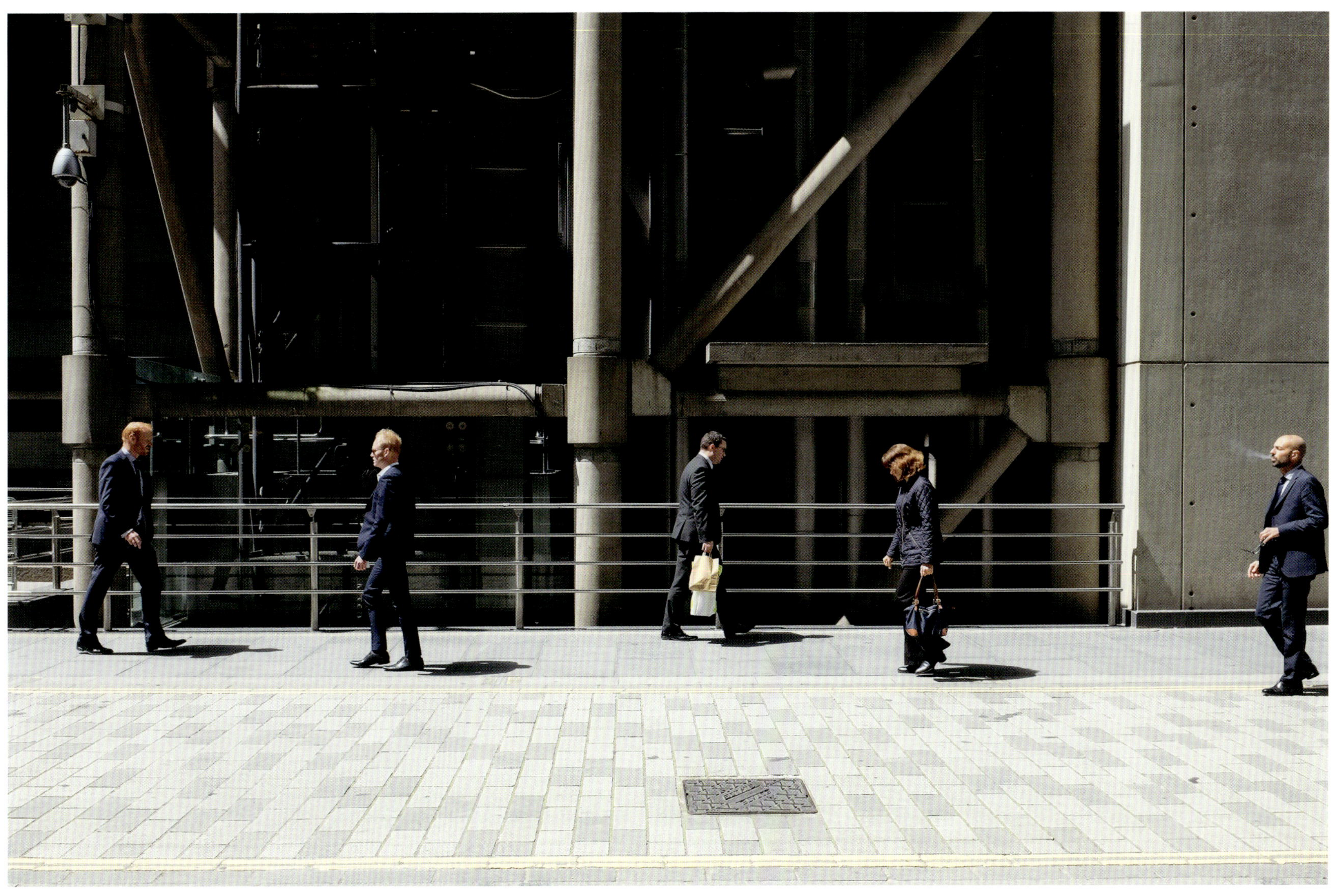

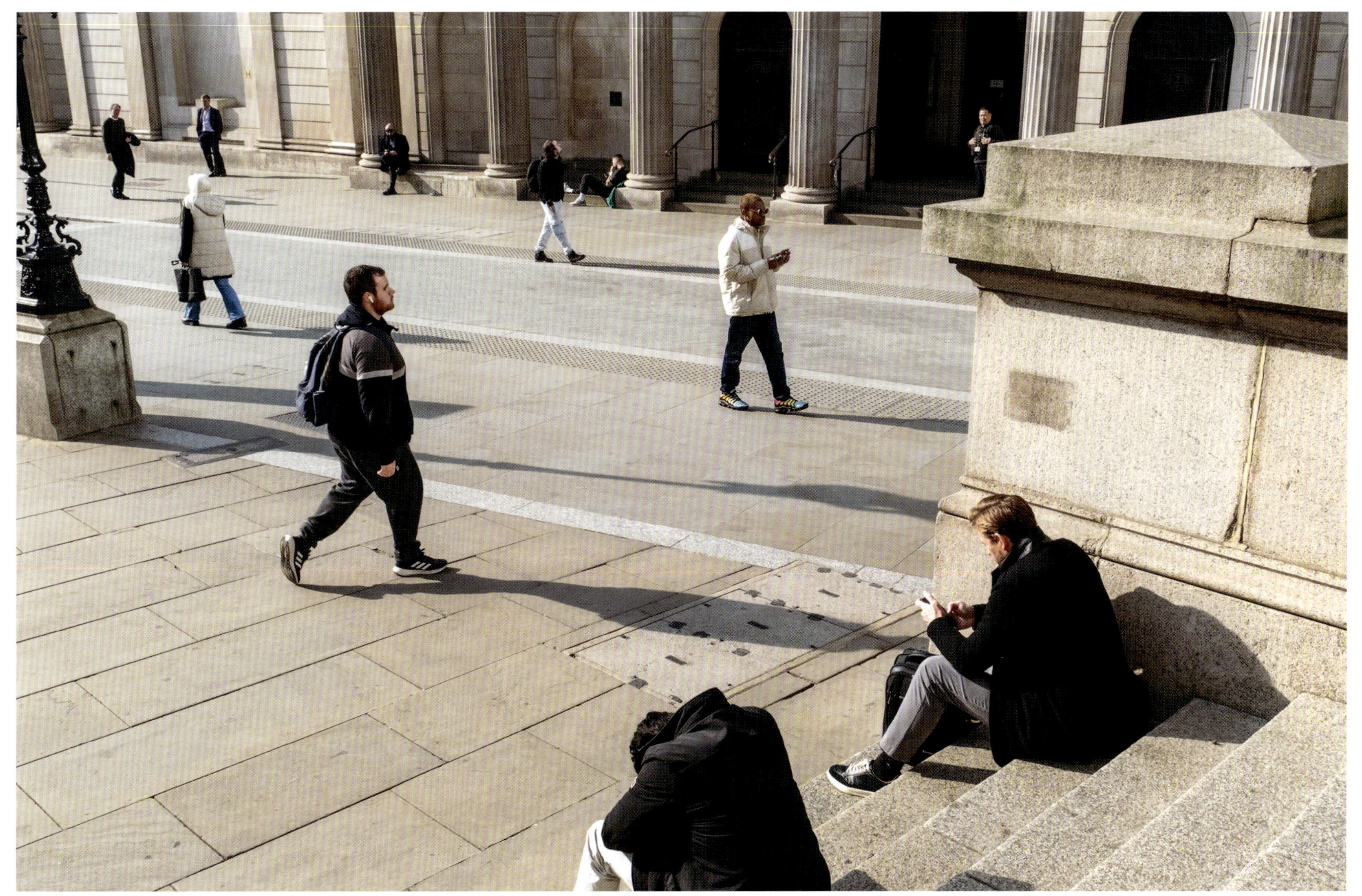

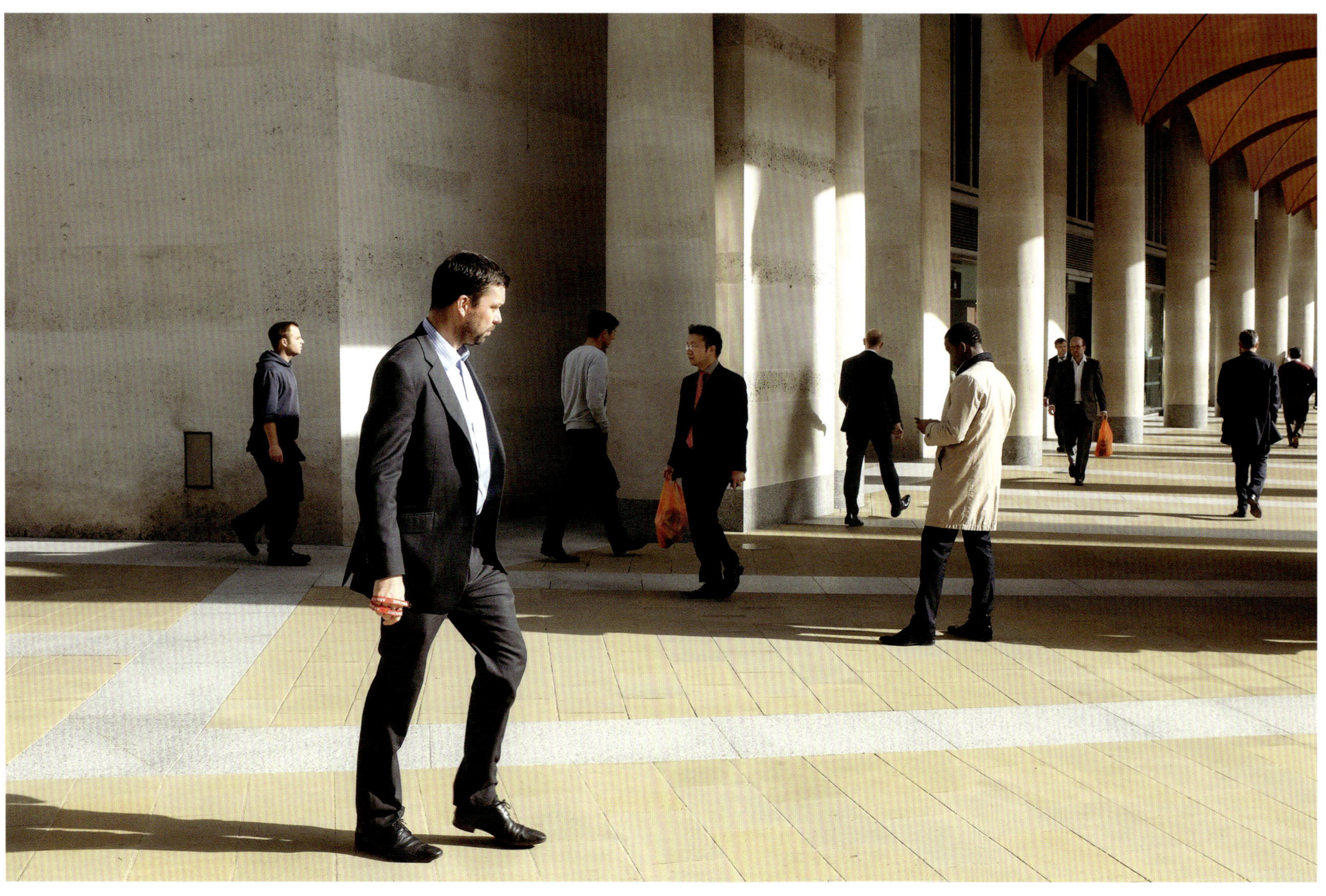

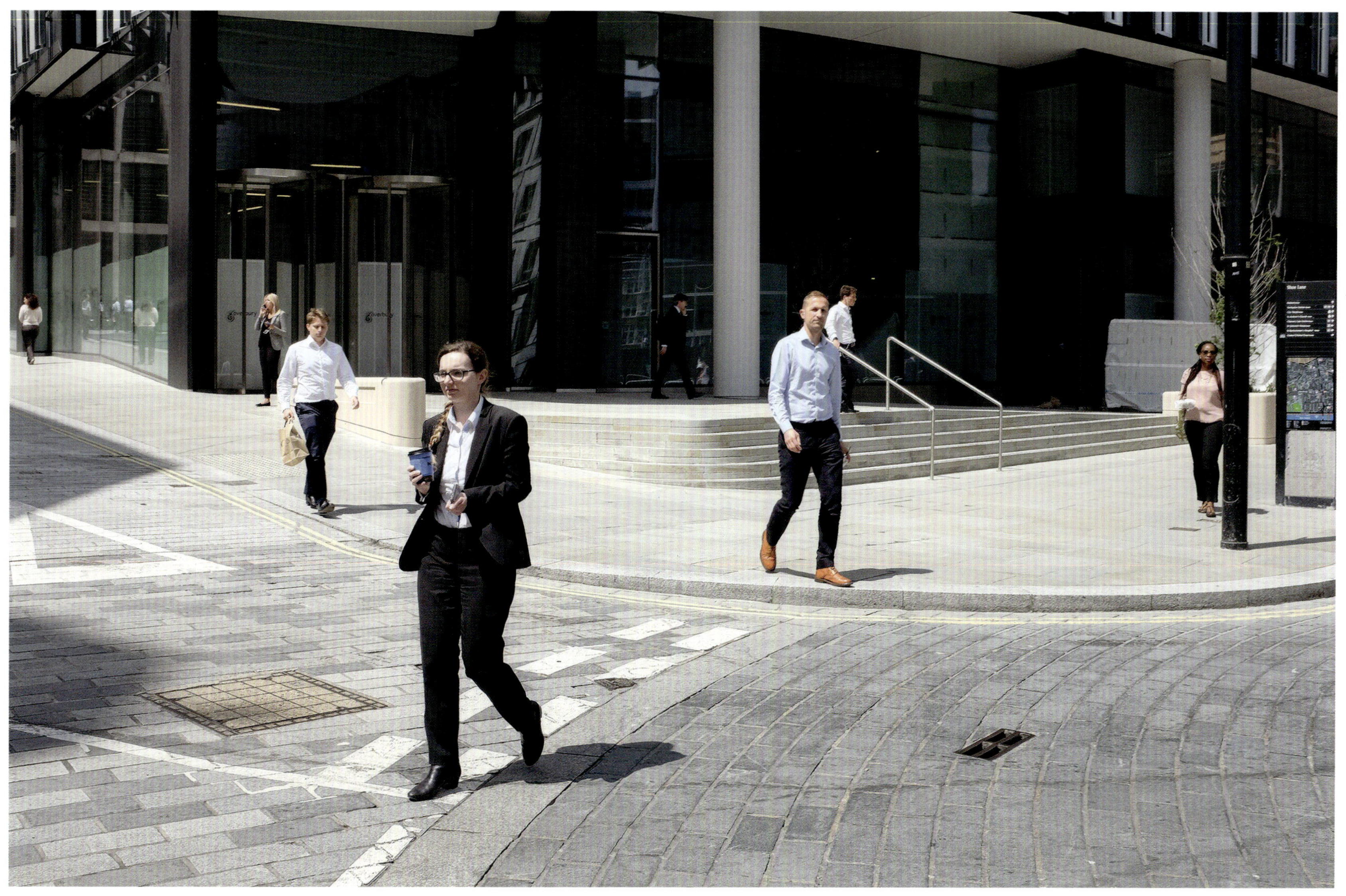

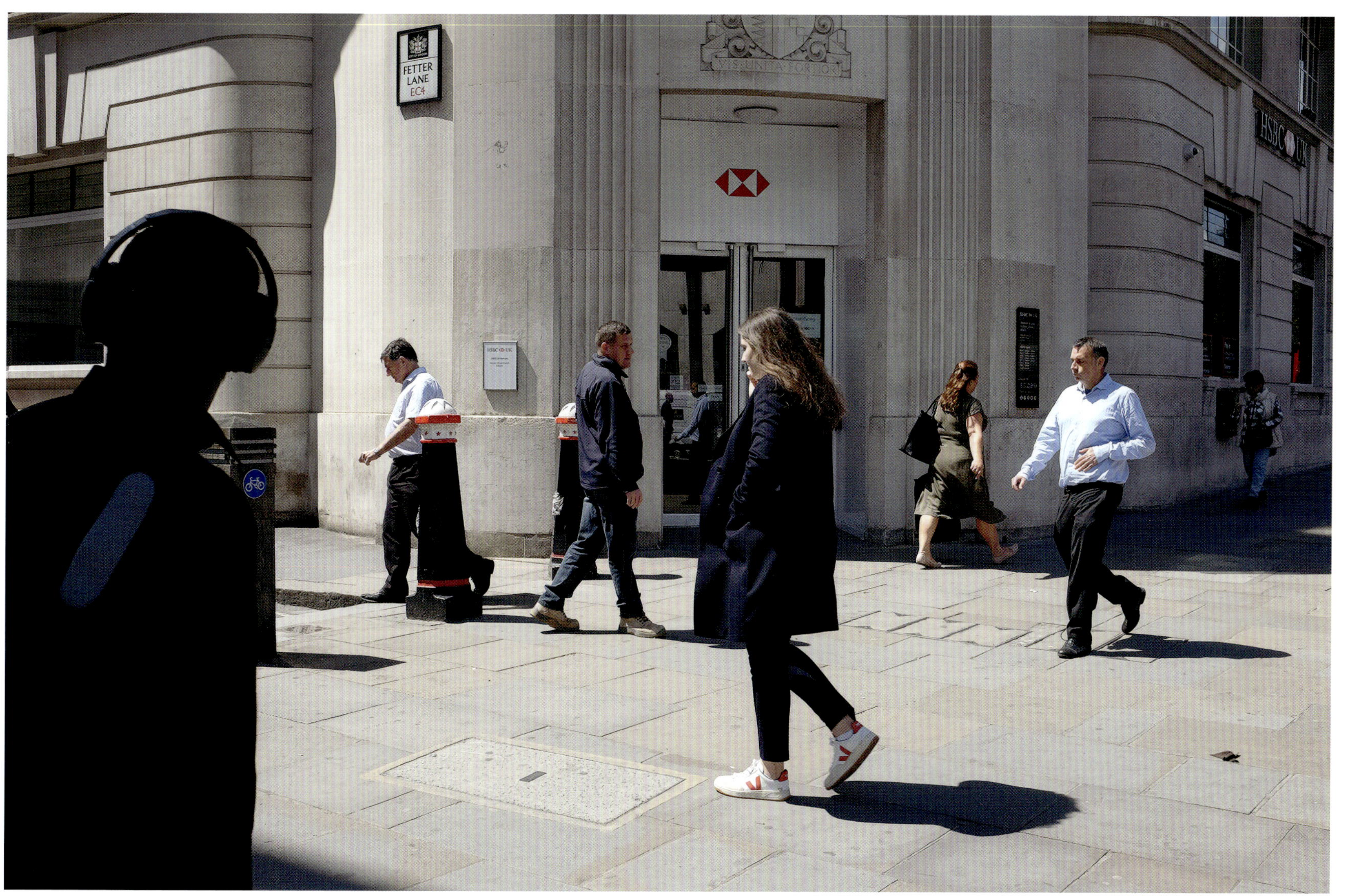
FETTER
LANE
EC4
VIS UNITA FORTIOR
HSBC UK

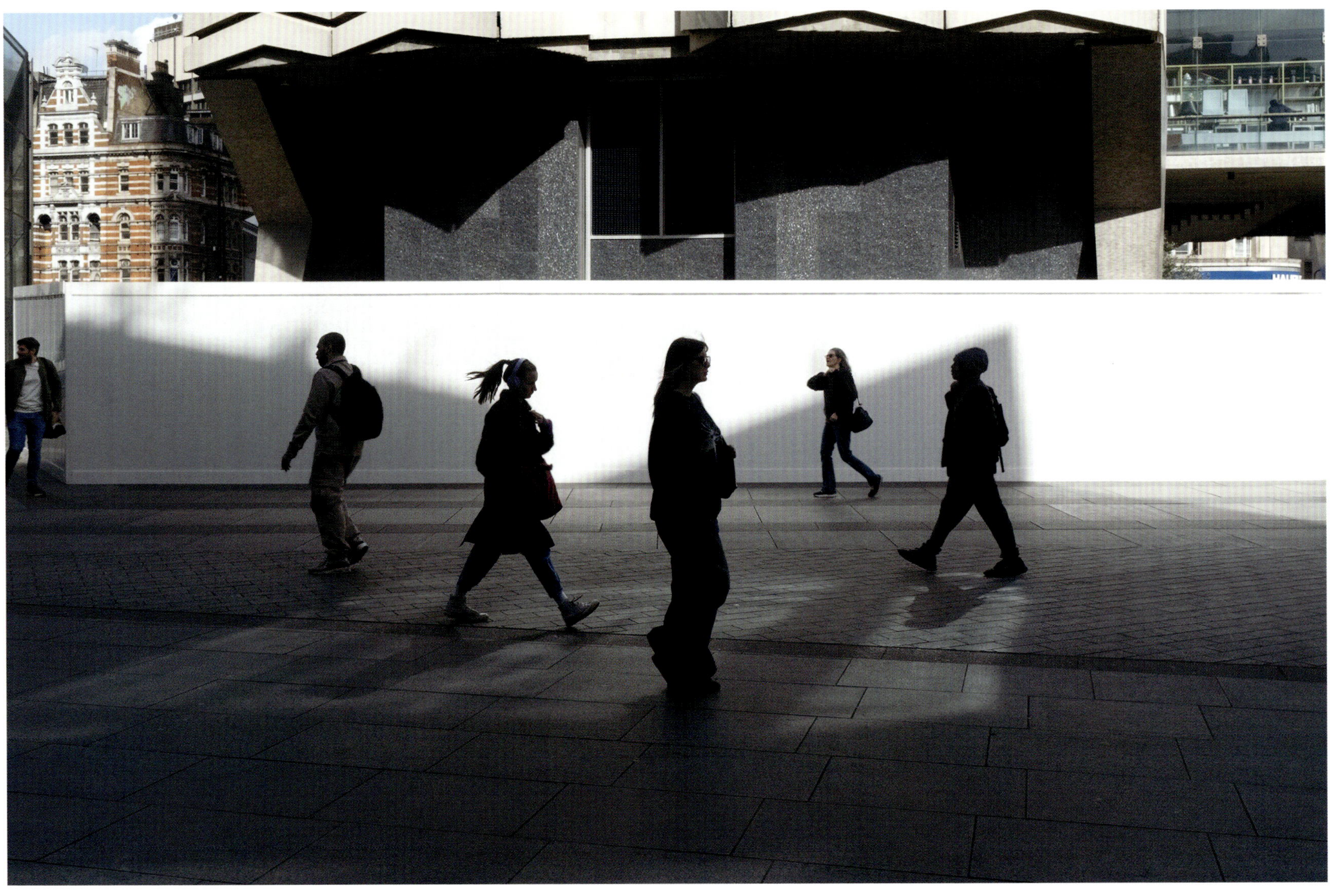

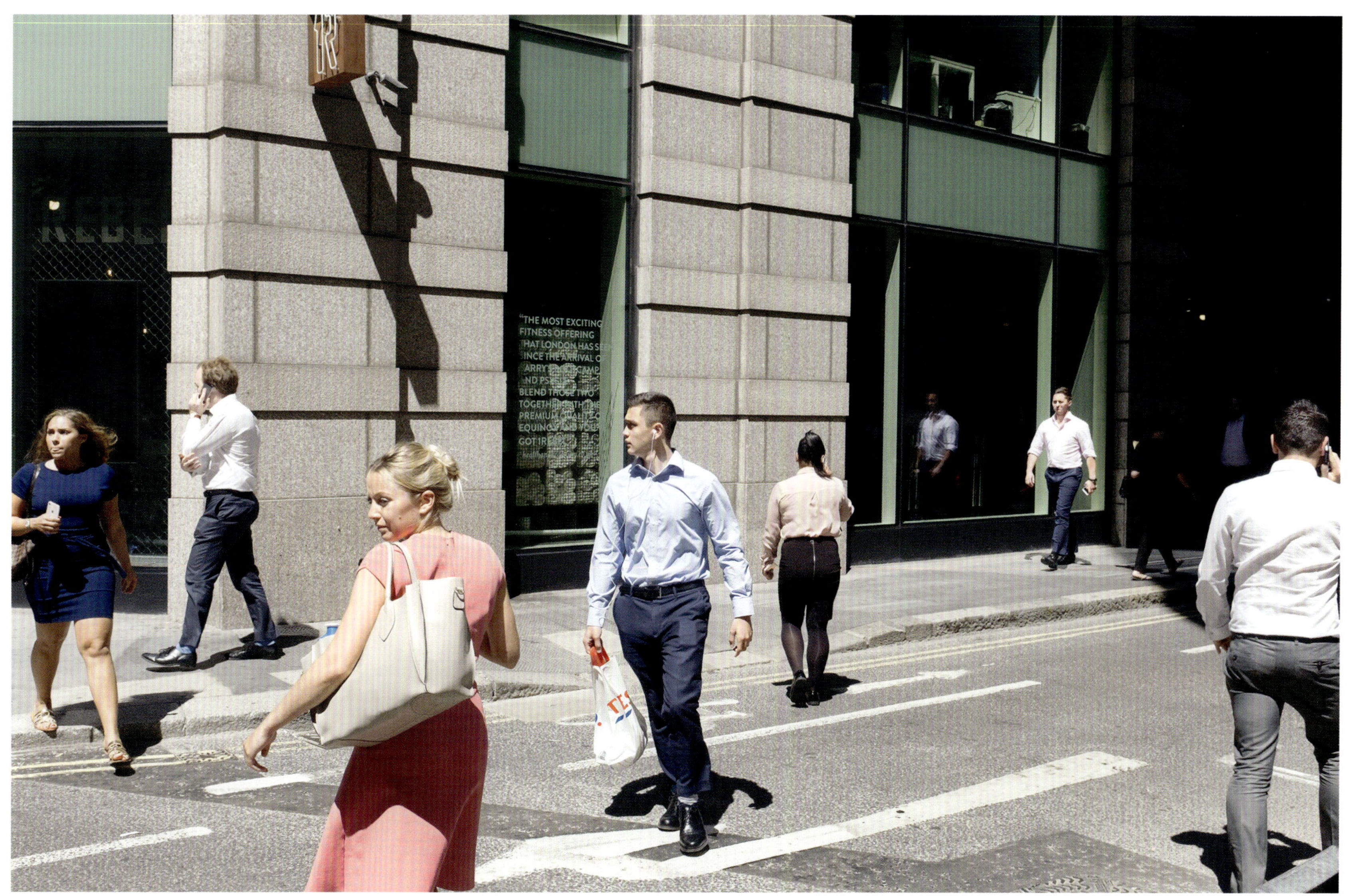

"THE MOST EXCITING
FITNESS OFFERING

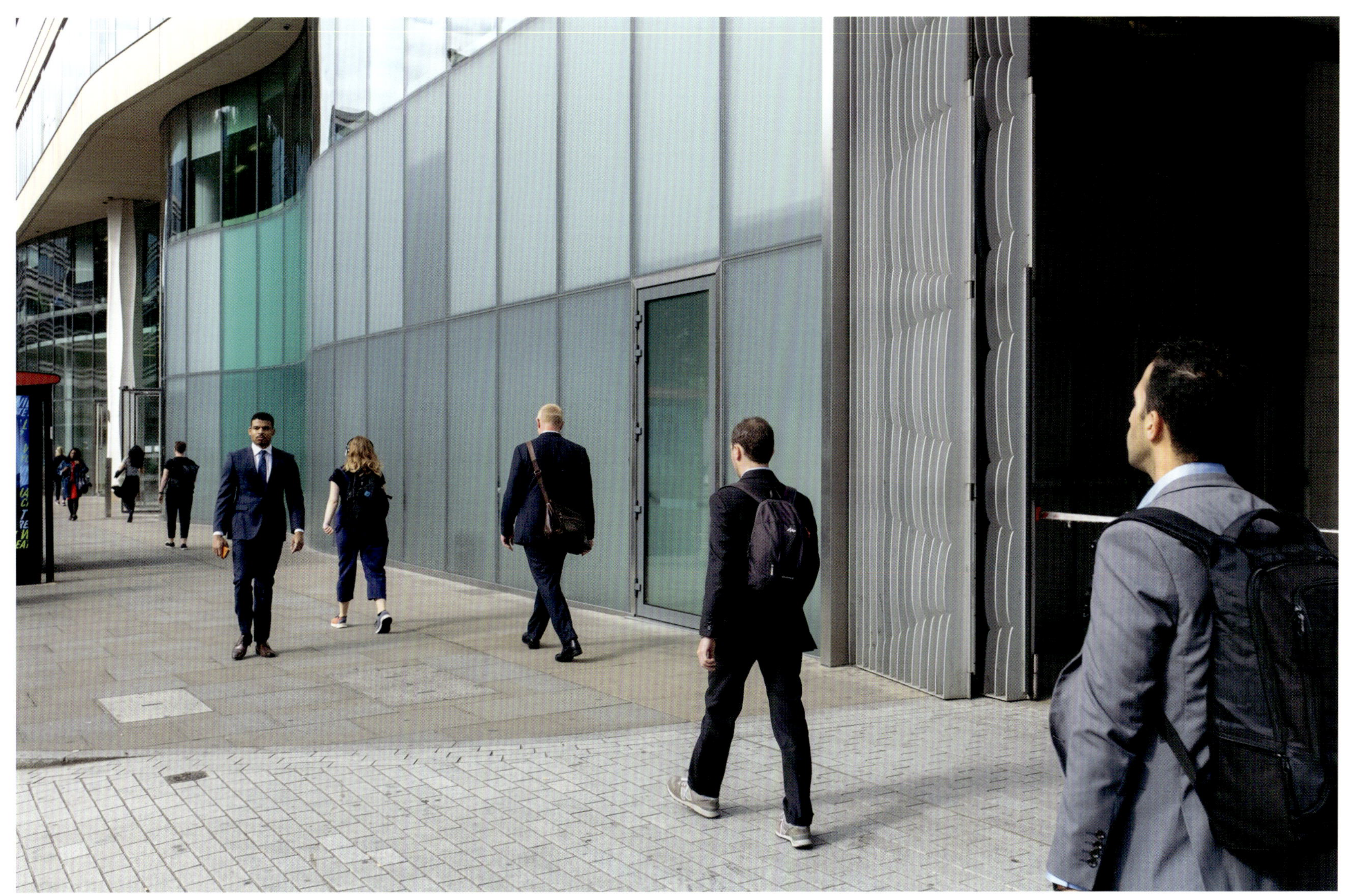

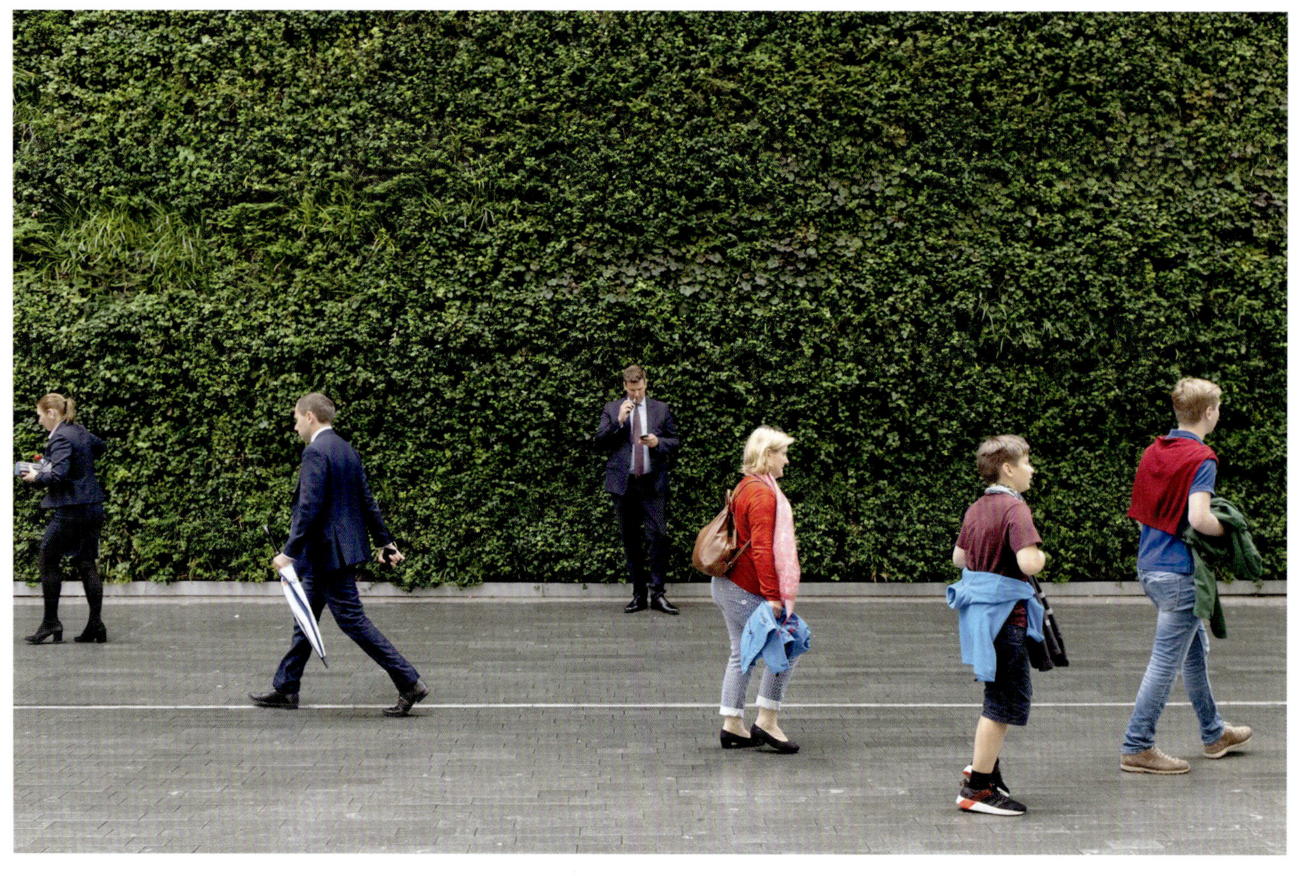

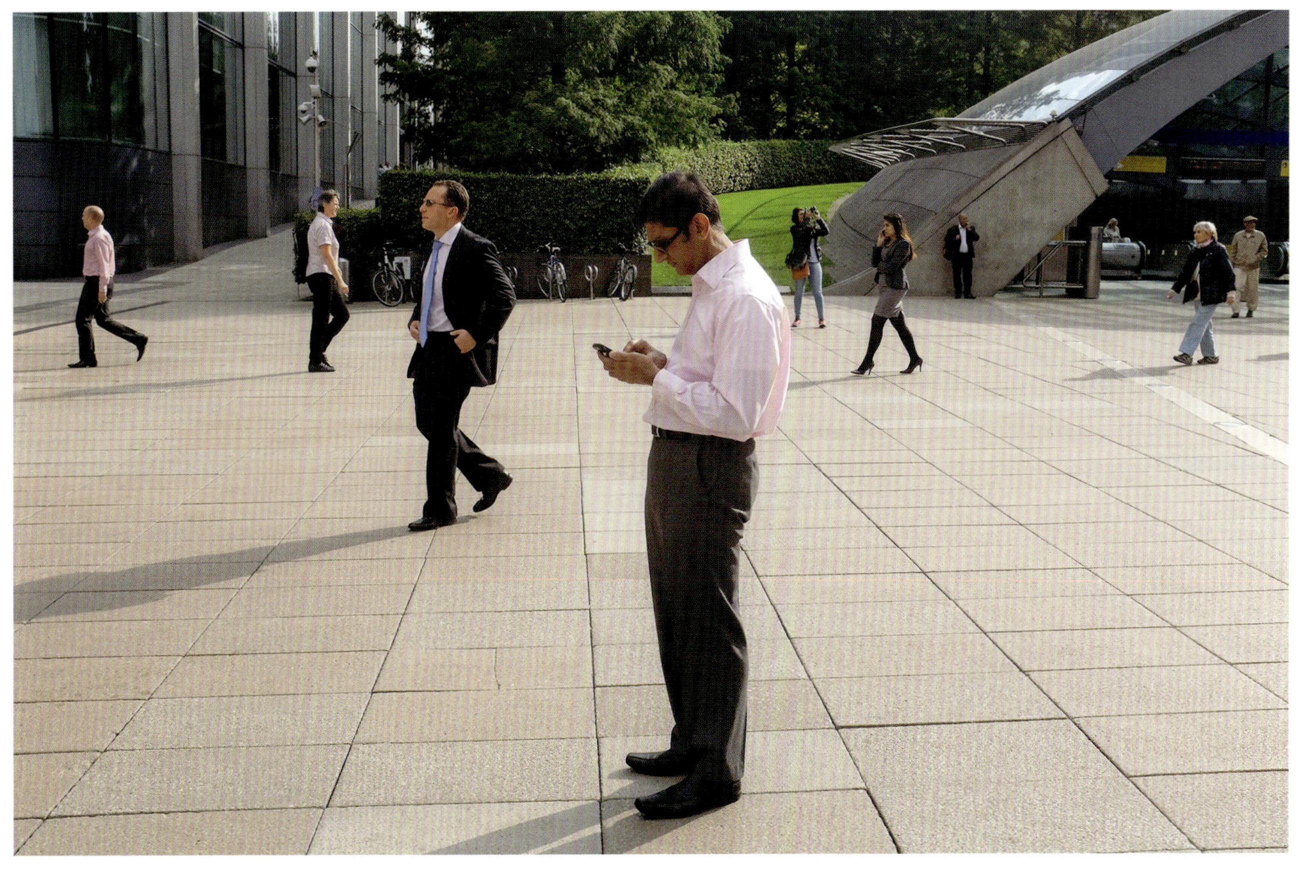

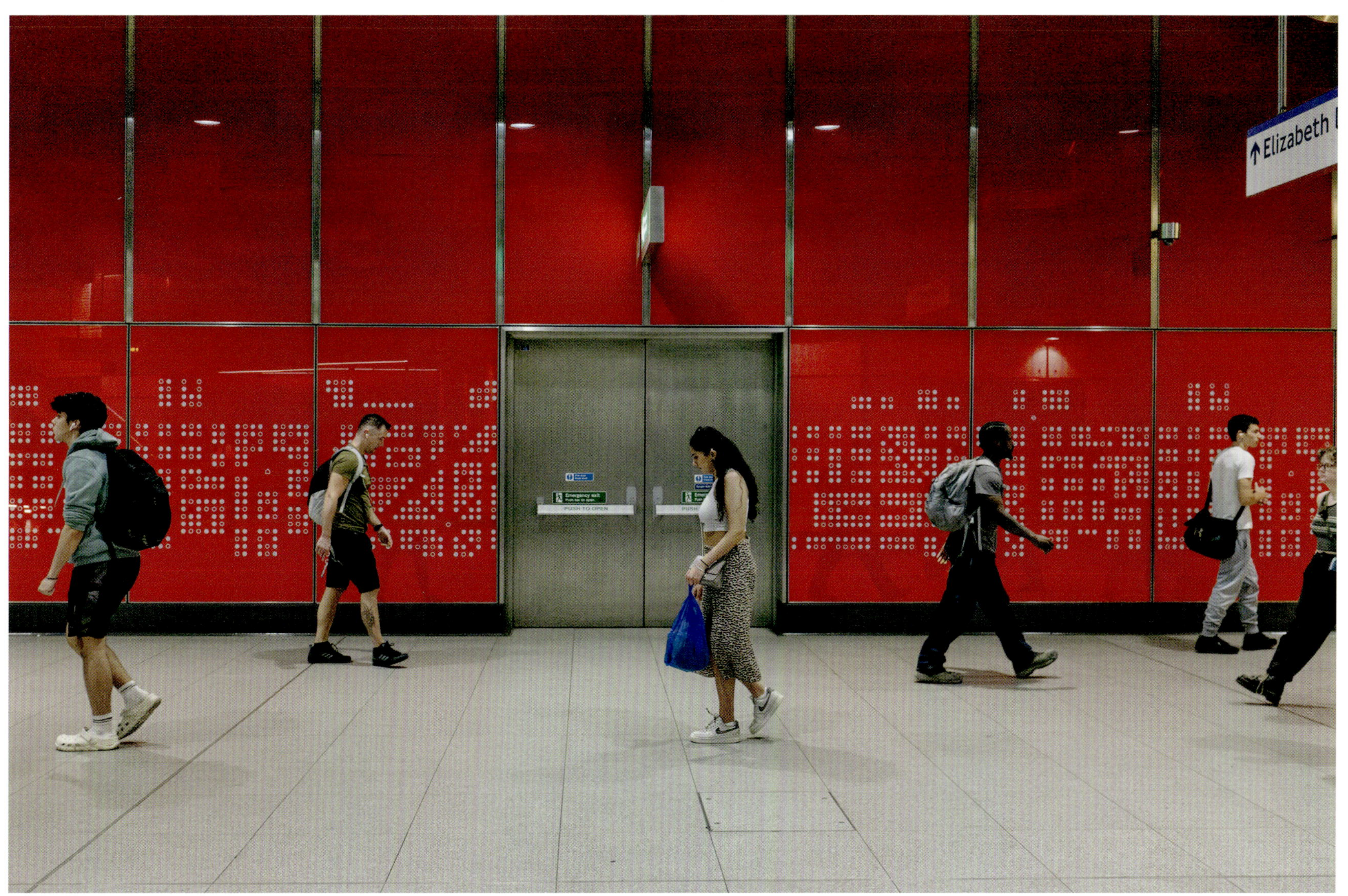
Elizabeth

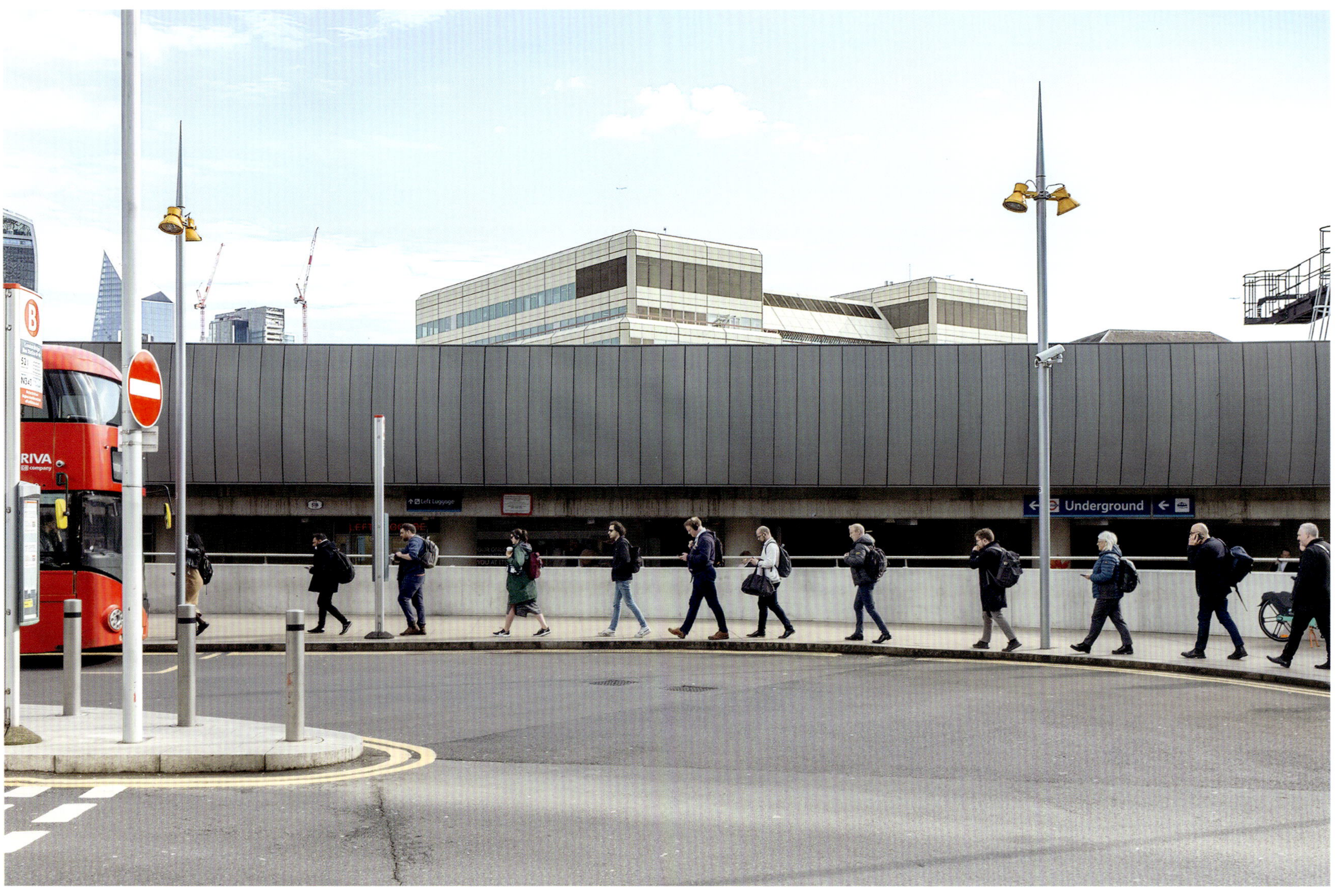
Underground

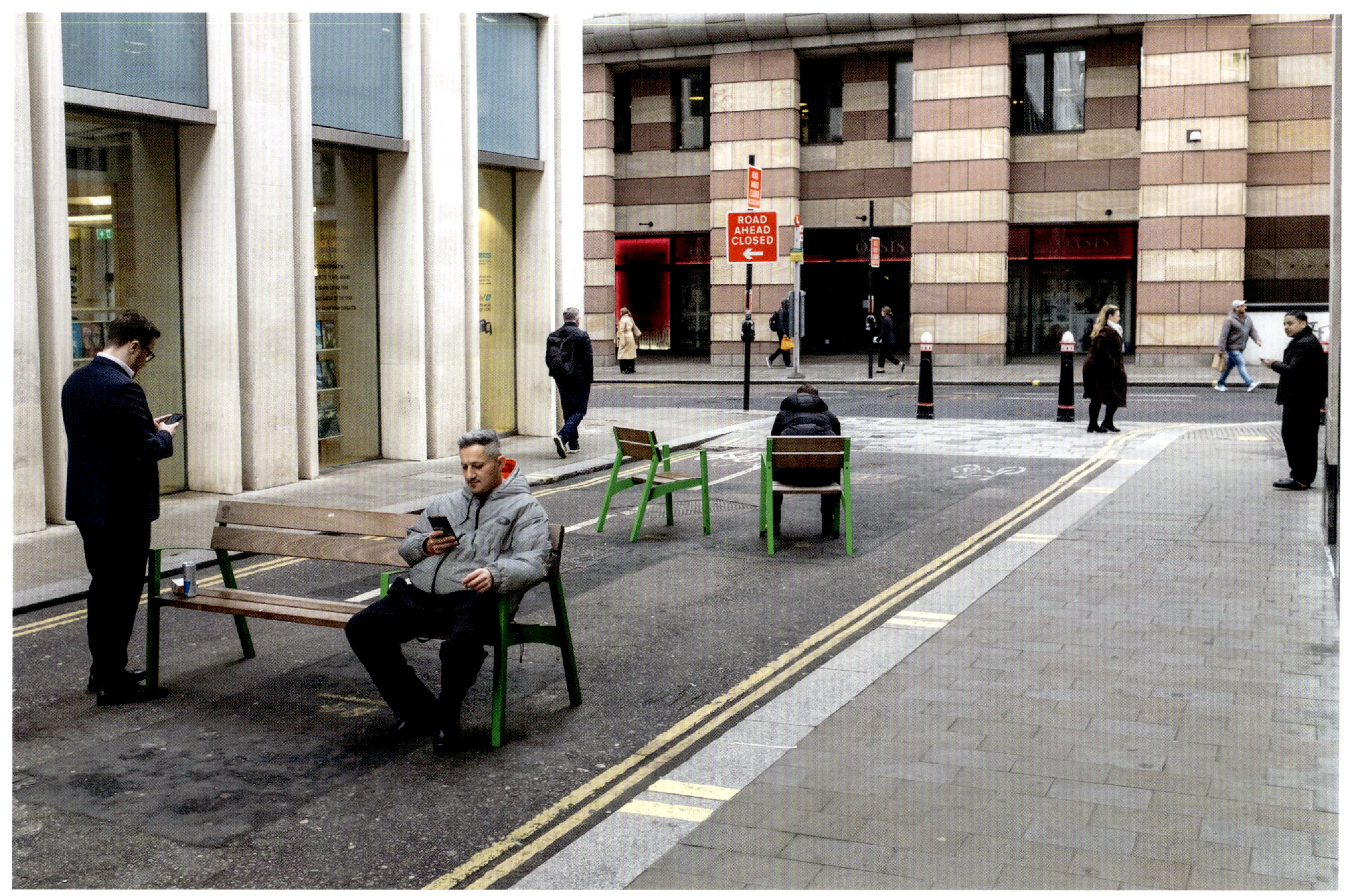
ROAD
AHEAD
CLOSED

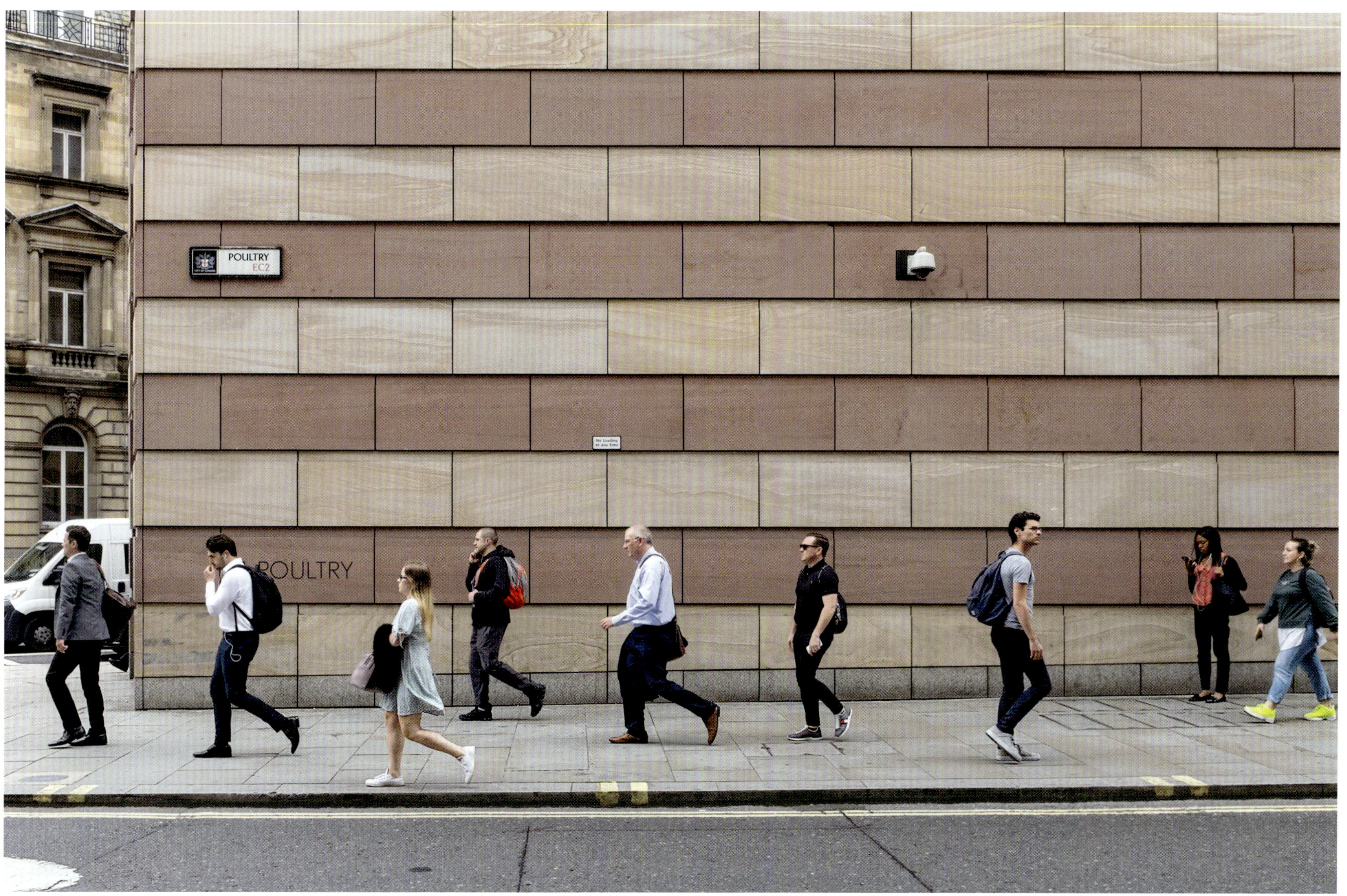
POULTRY
EC2
POULTRY

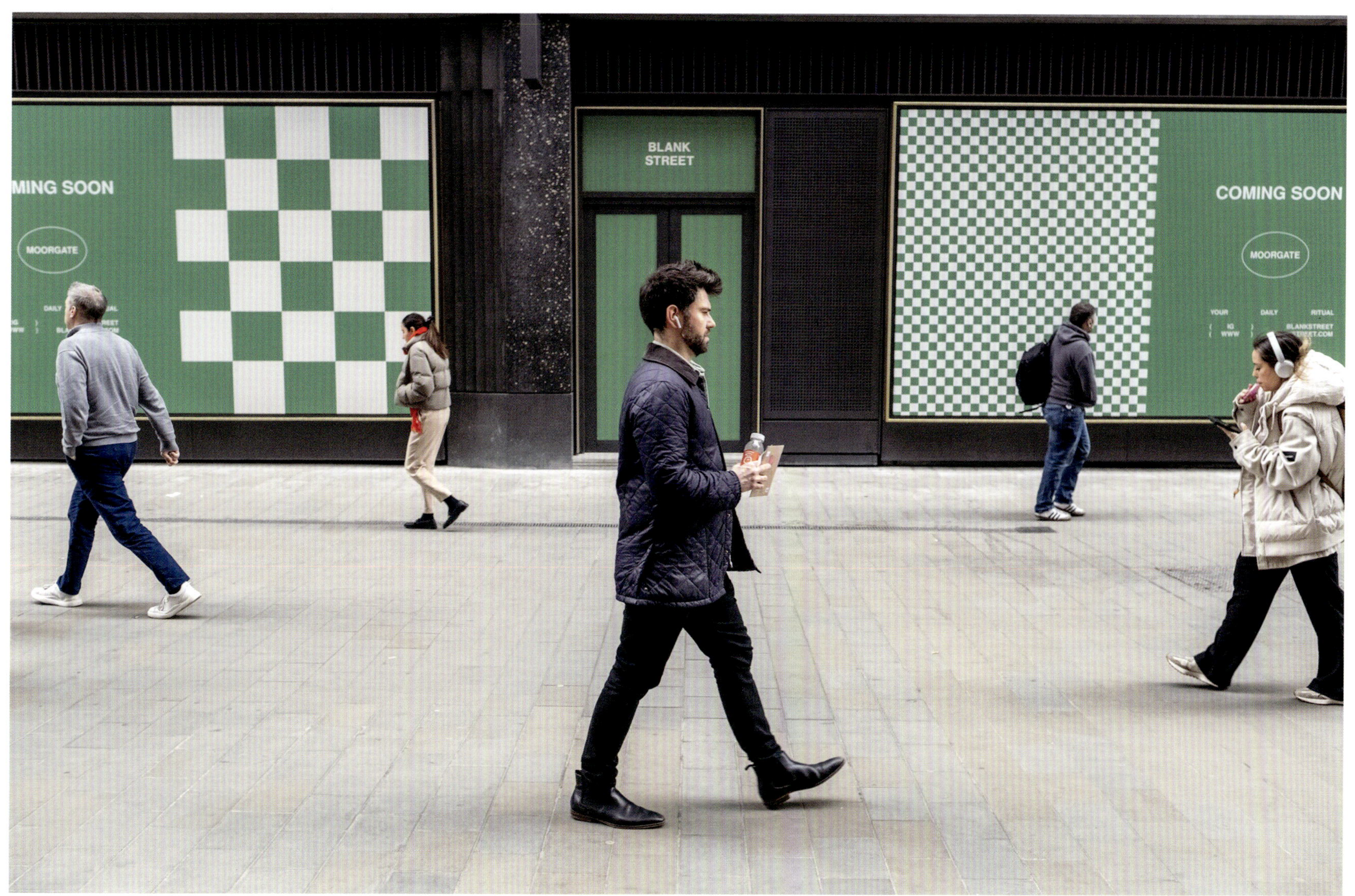
MING SOON
MOORGATE
BLANK
STREET
COMING SOON
MOORGATE
YOUR
DAILY
RITUAL

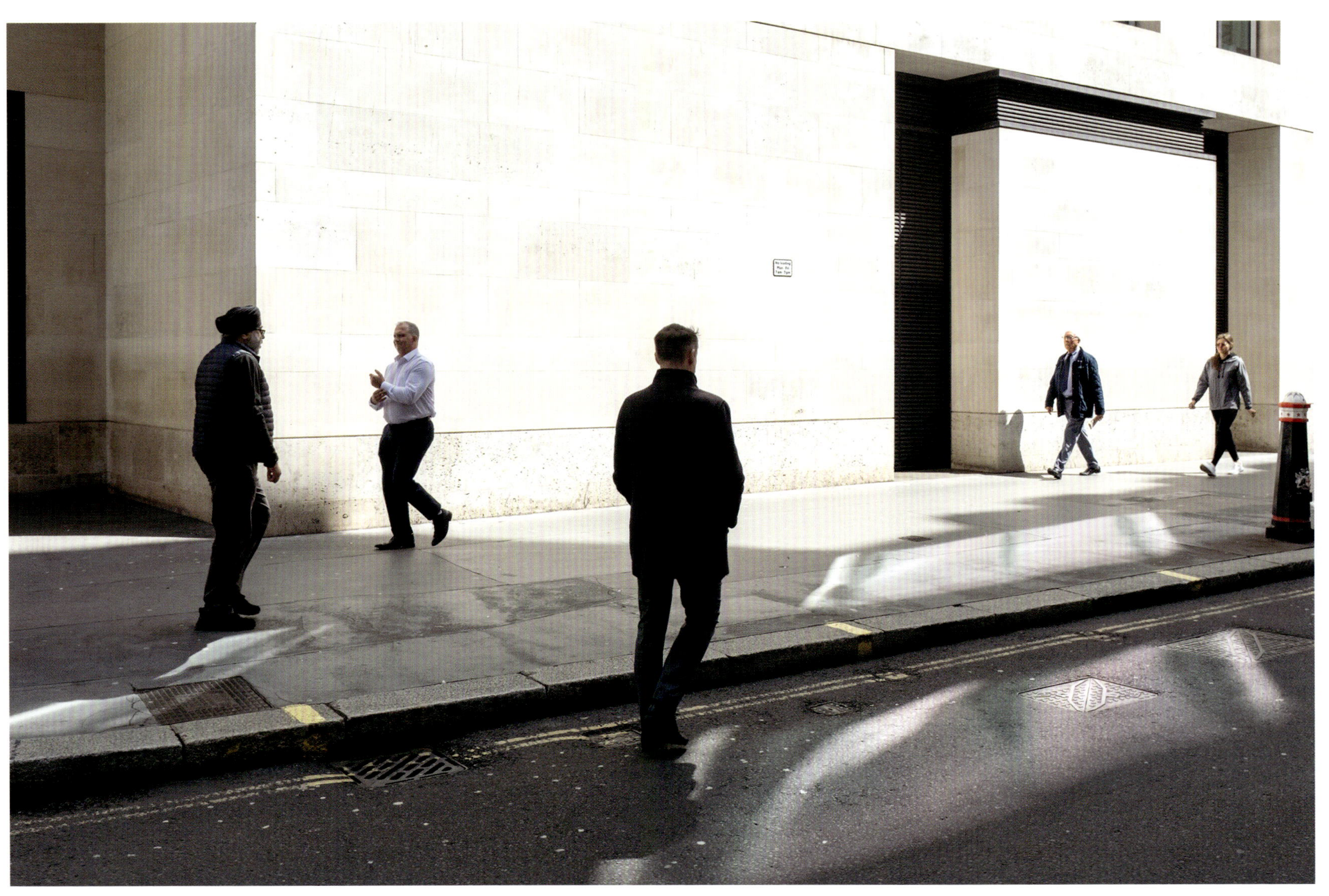

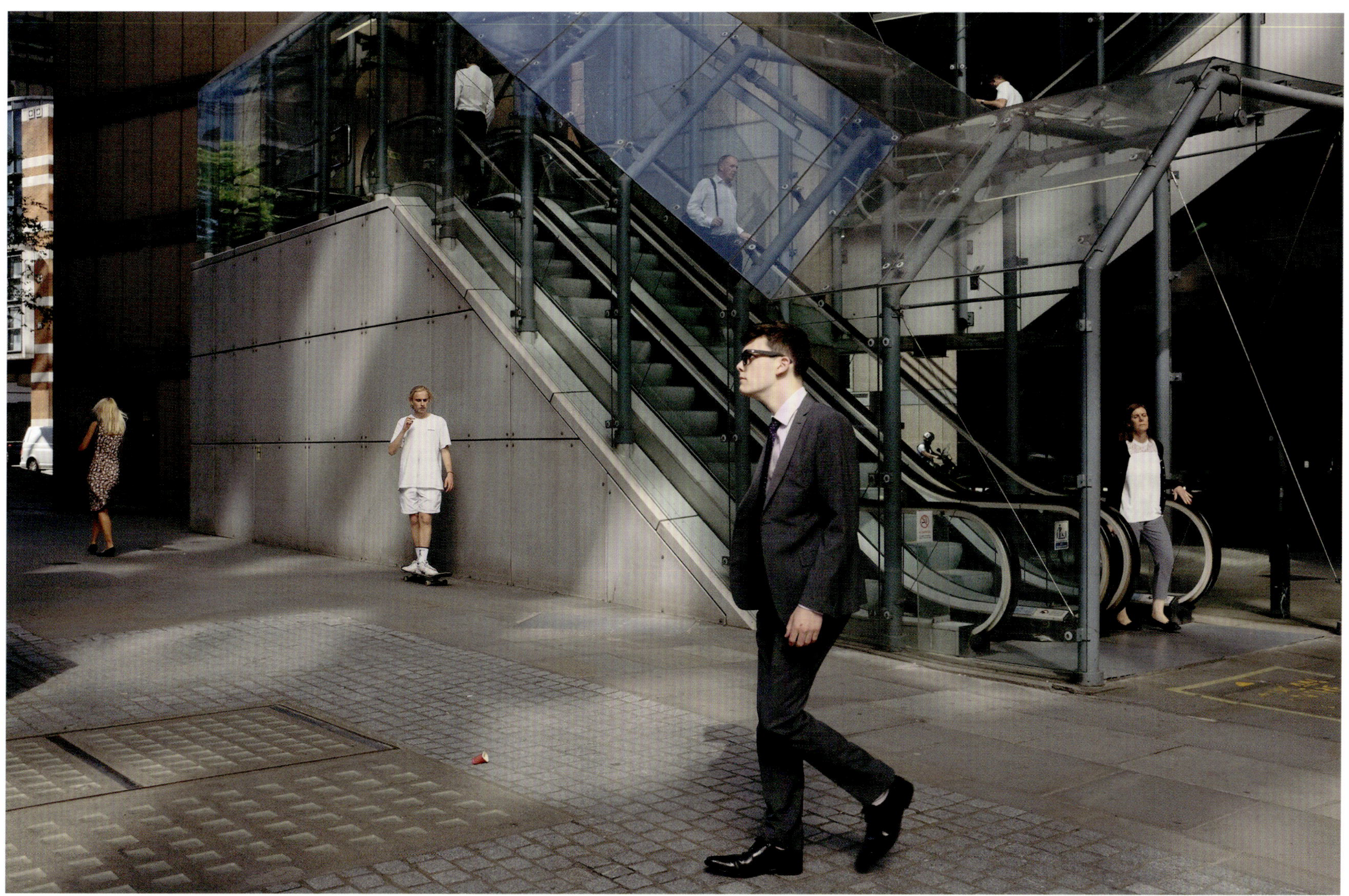

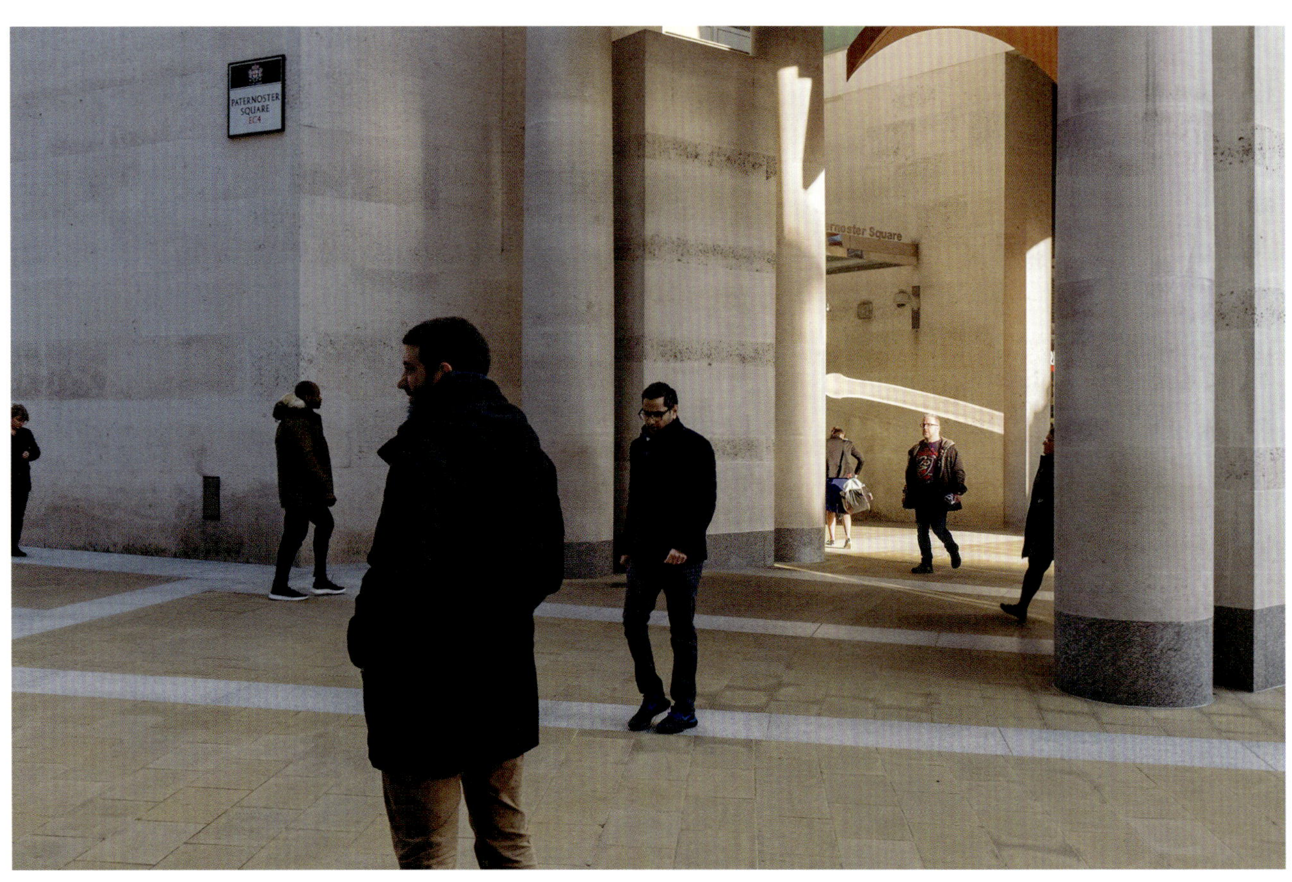
PATERNOSTER
SQUARE
EC4

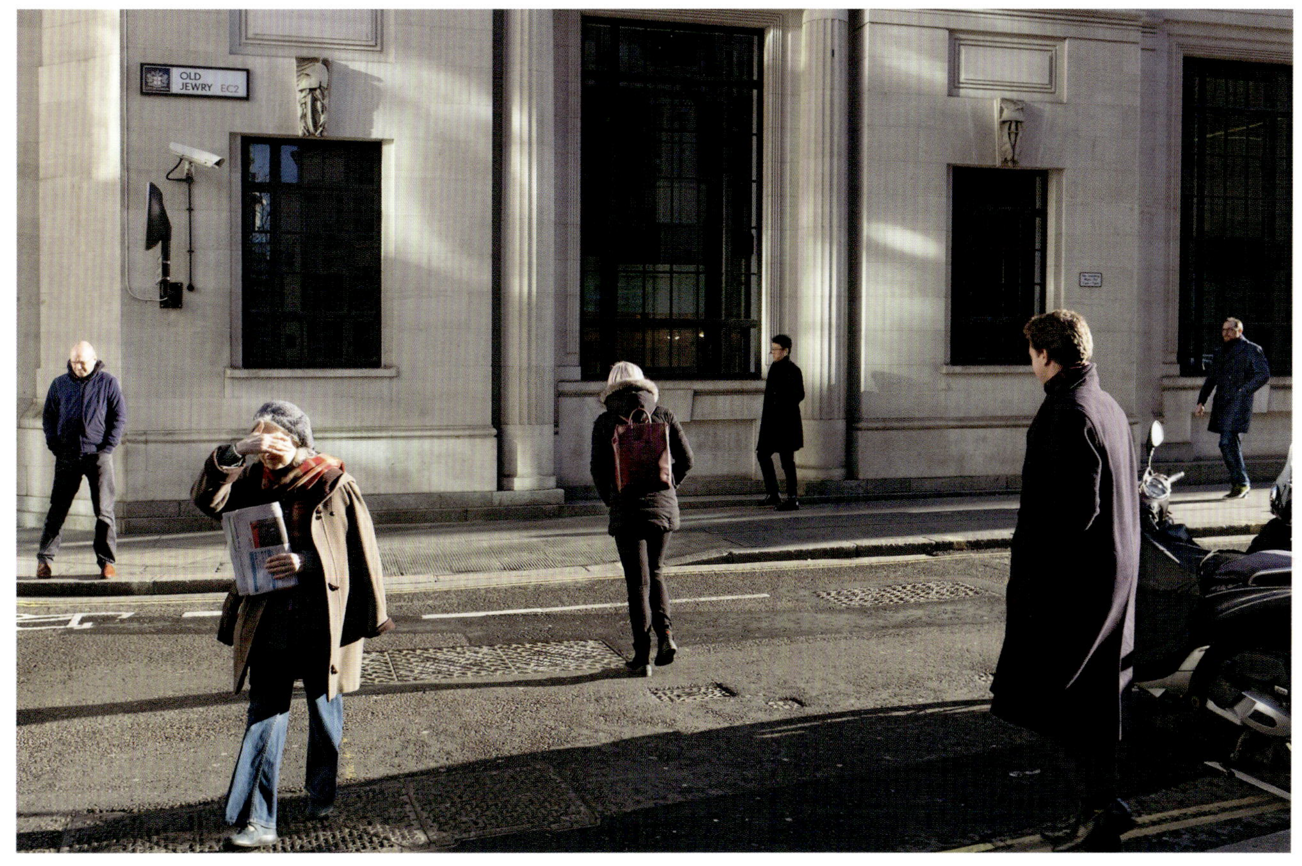
OLD
JEWRY EC2

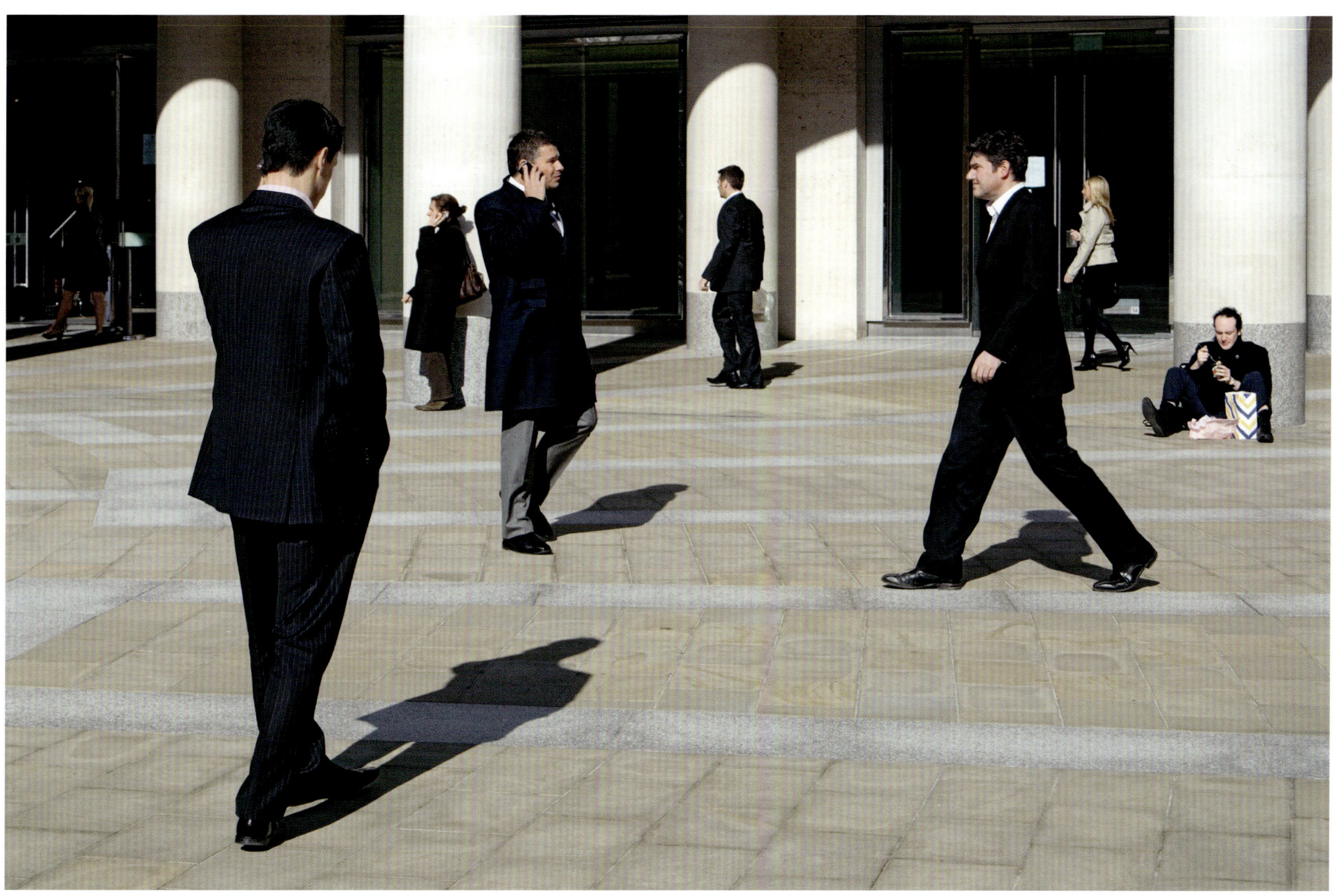

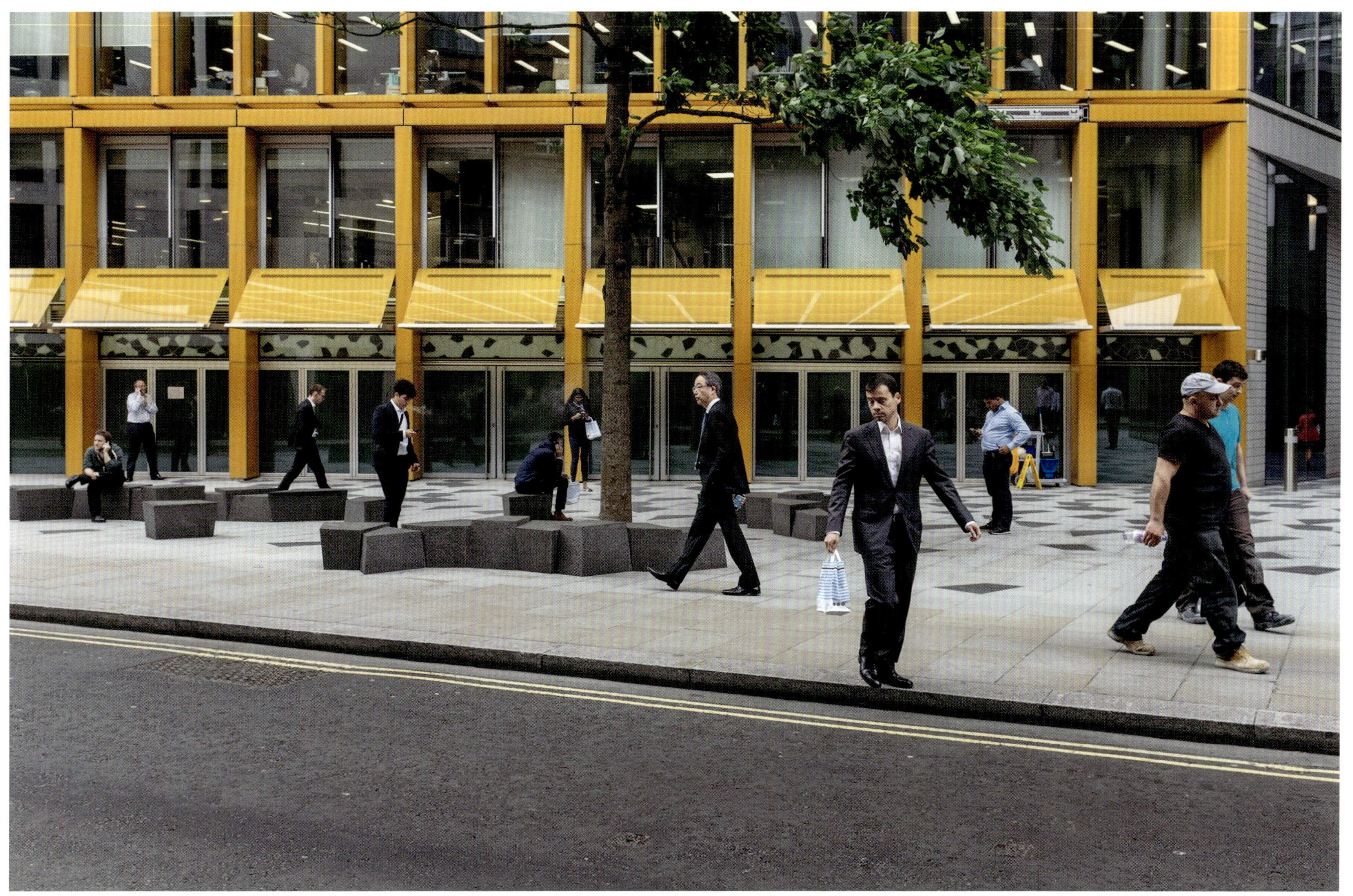

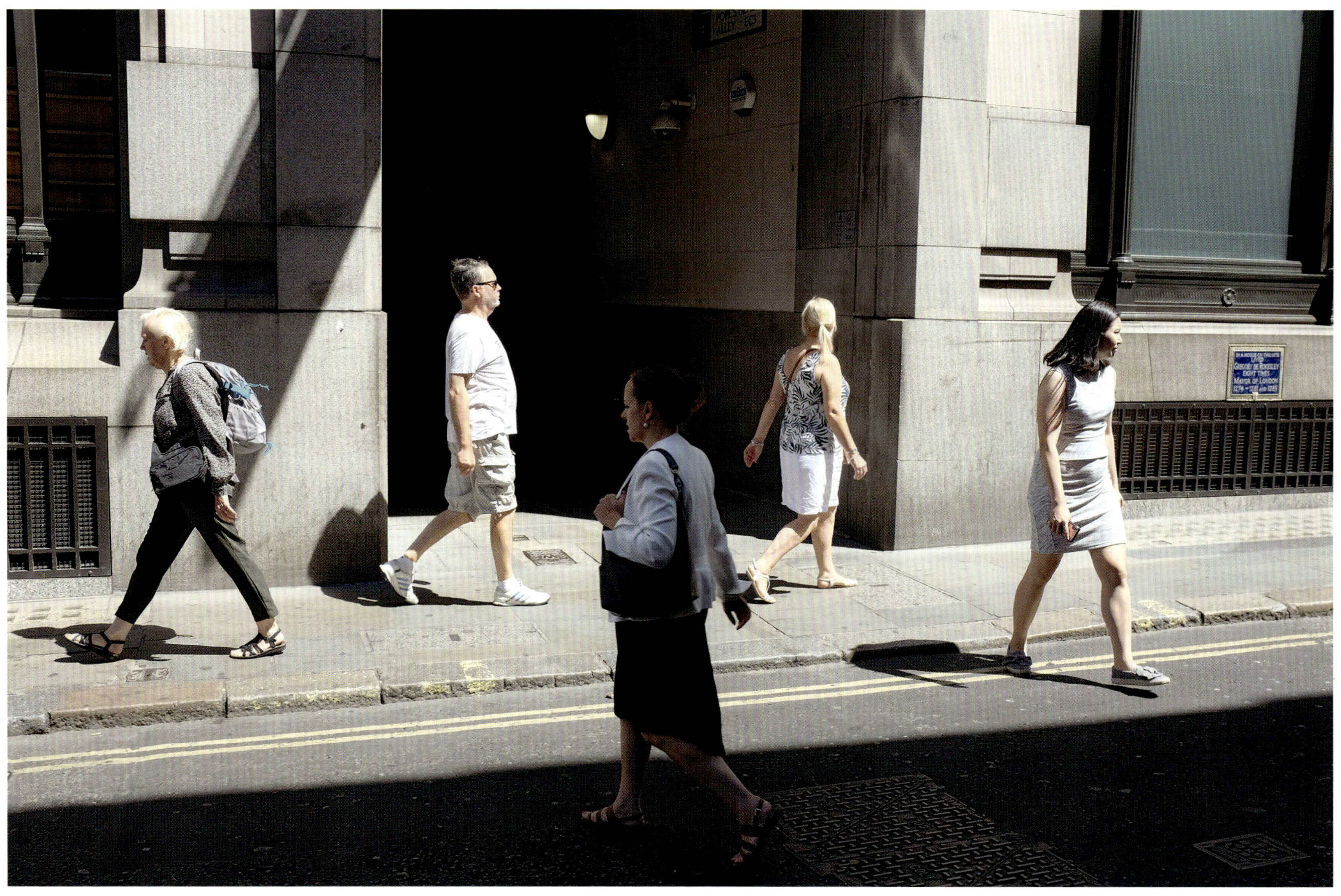
ALLEY EC3
LIVED
EIGHT TIMES
MAYOR OF LONDON

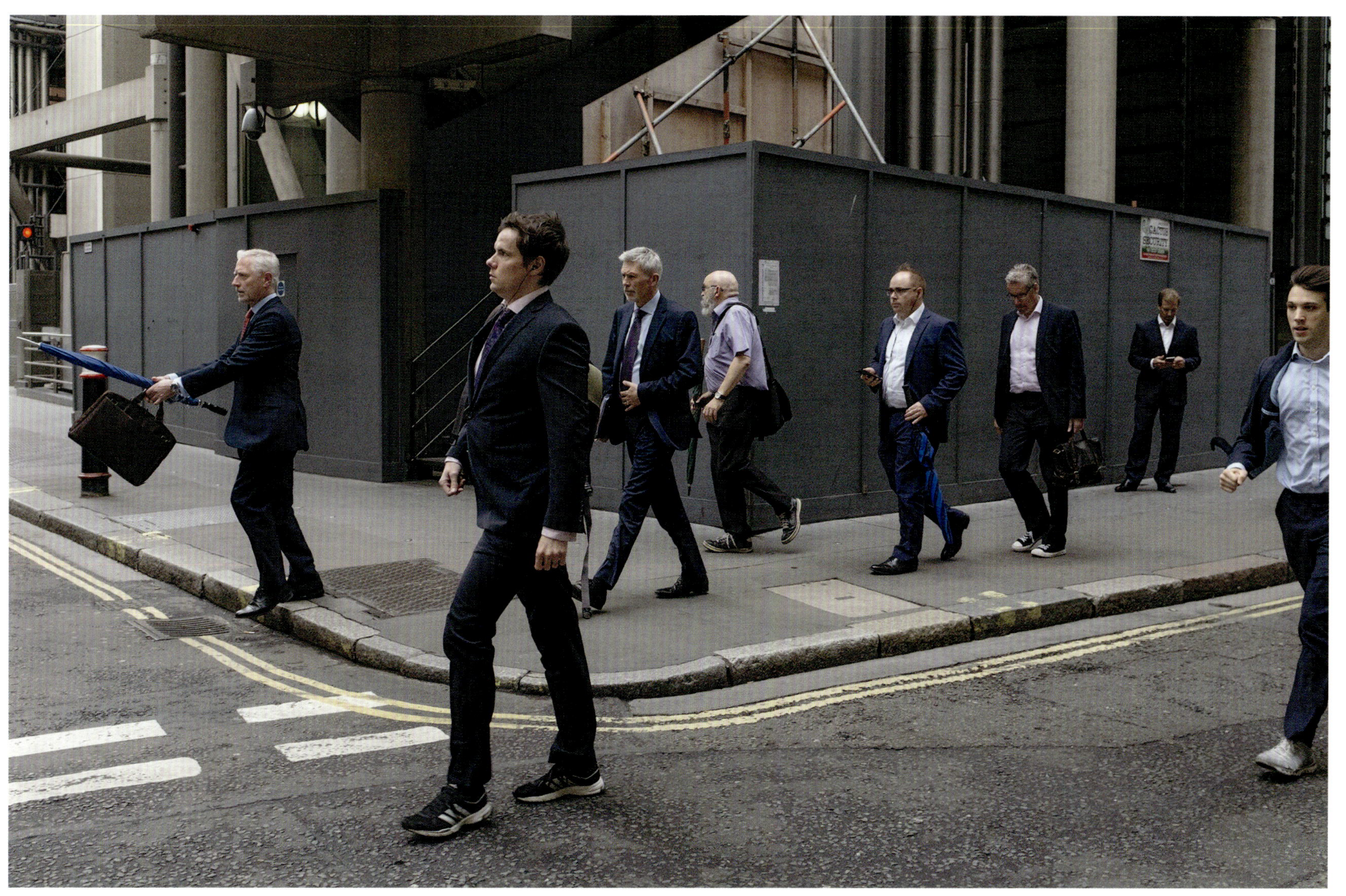

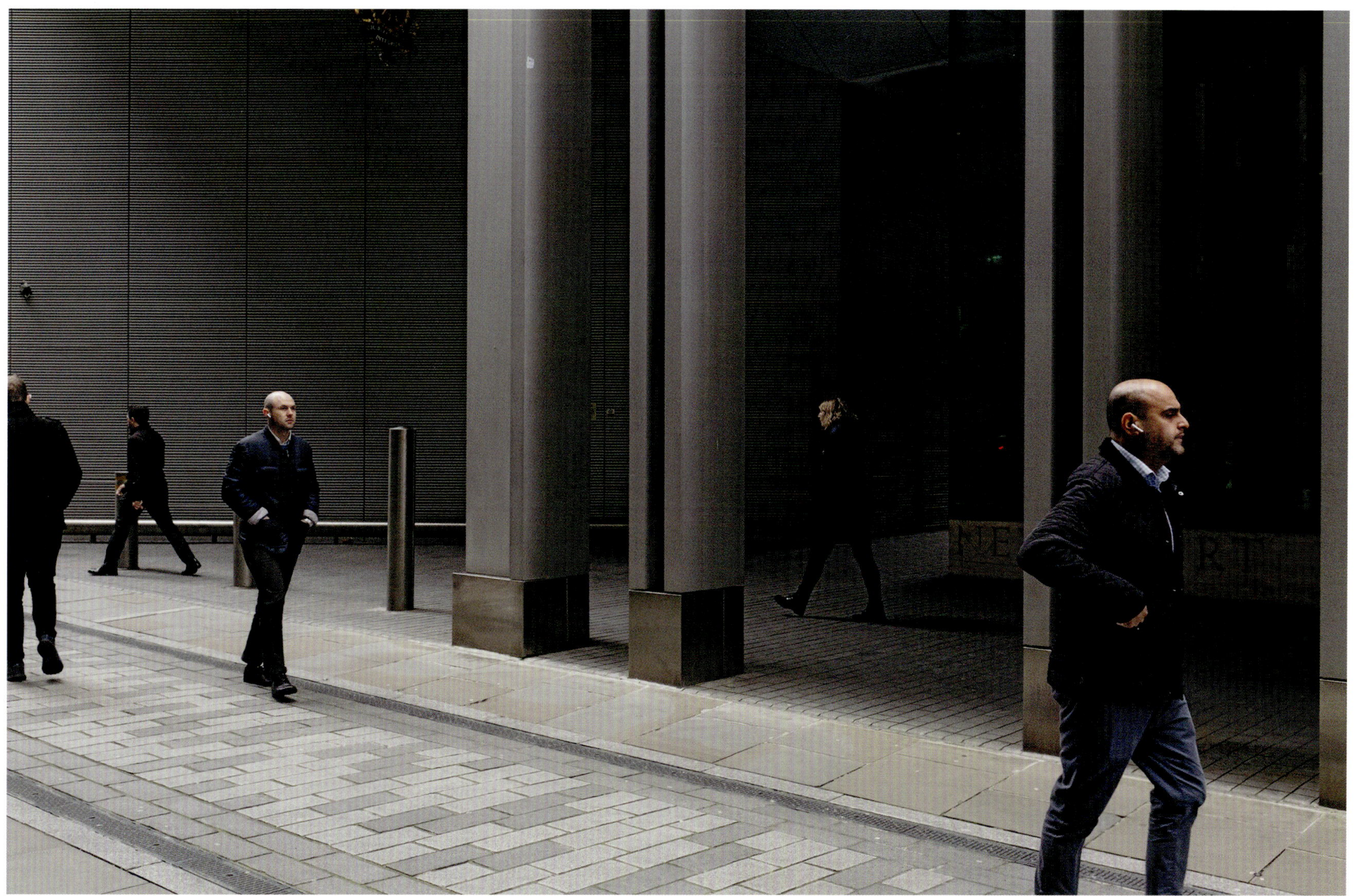

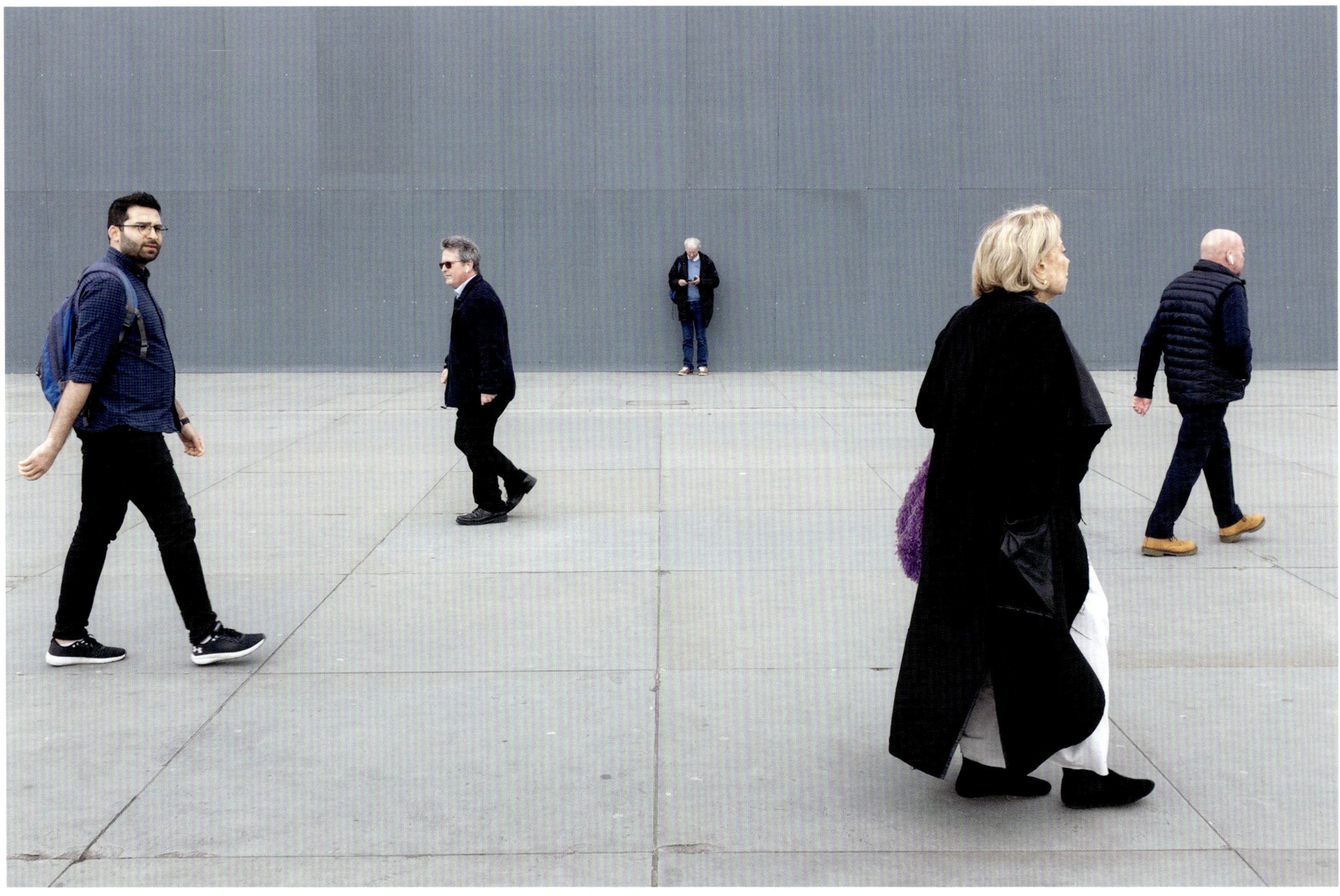

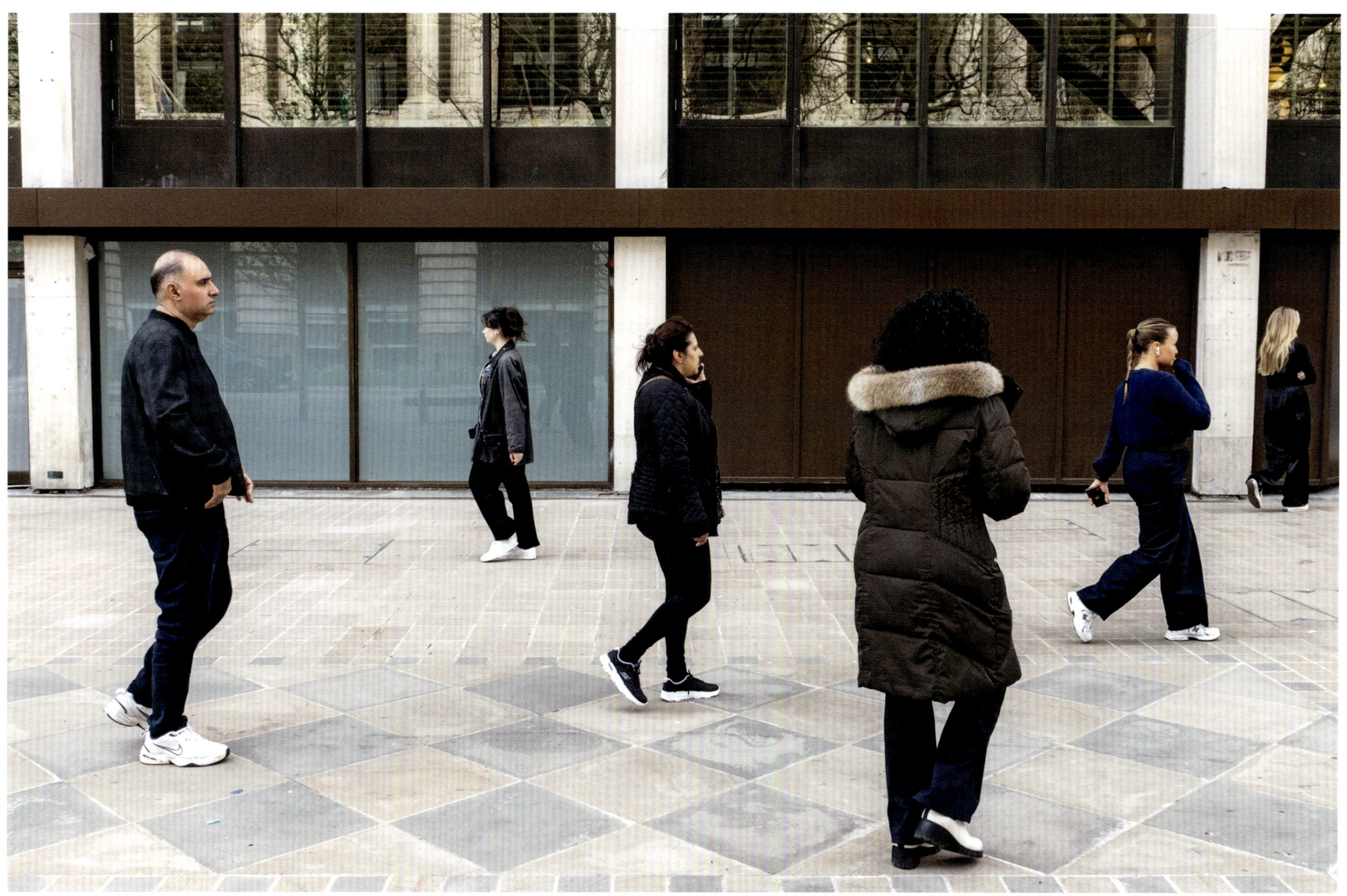

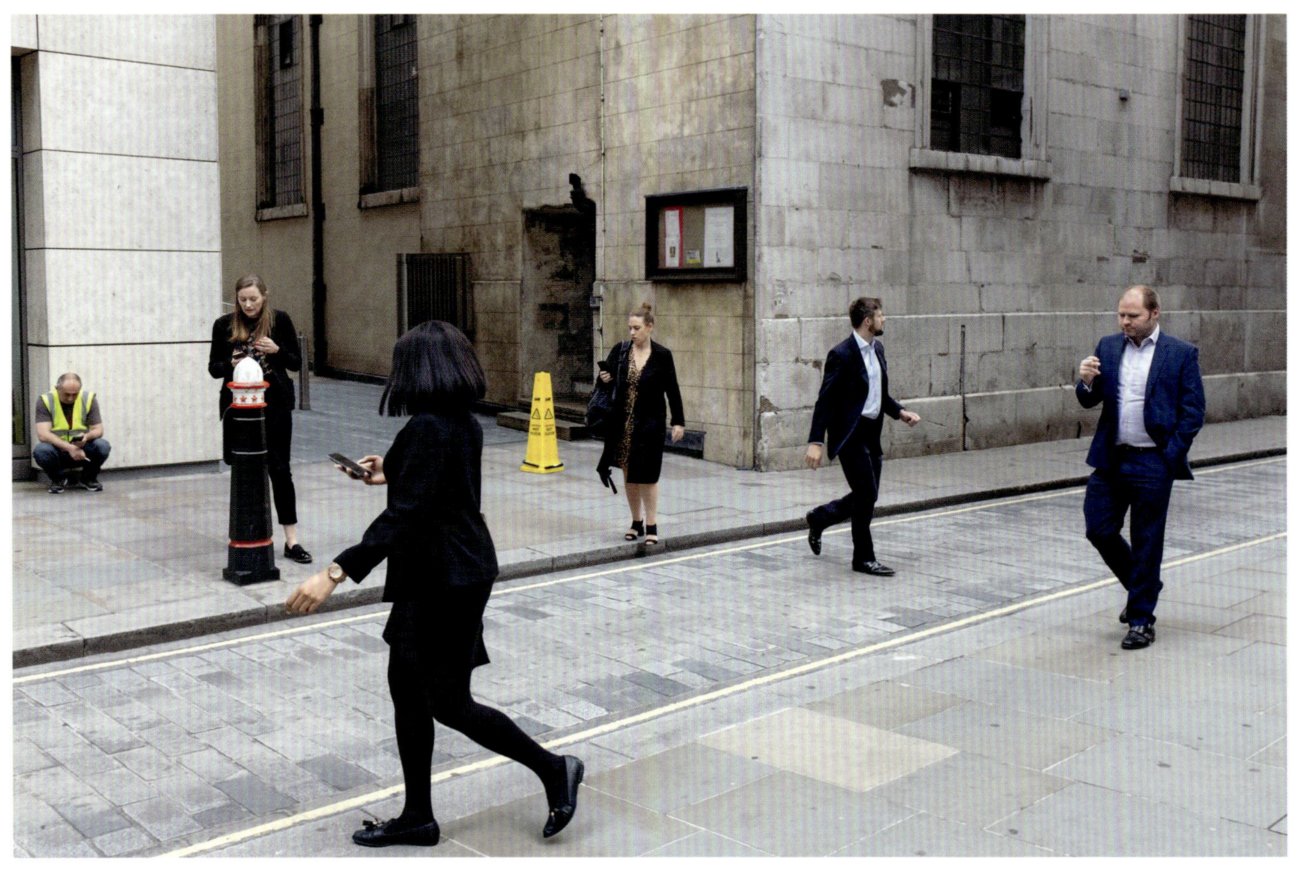

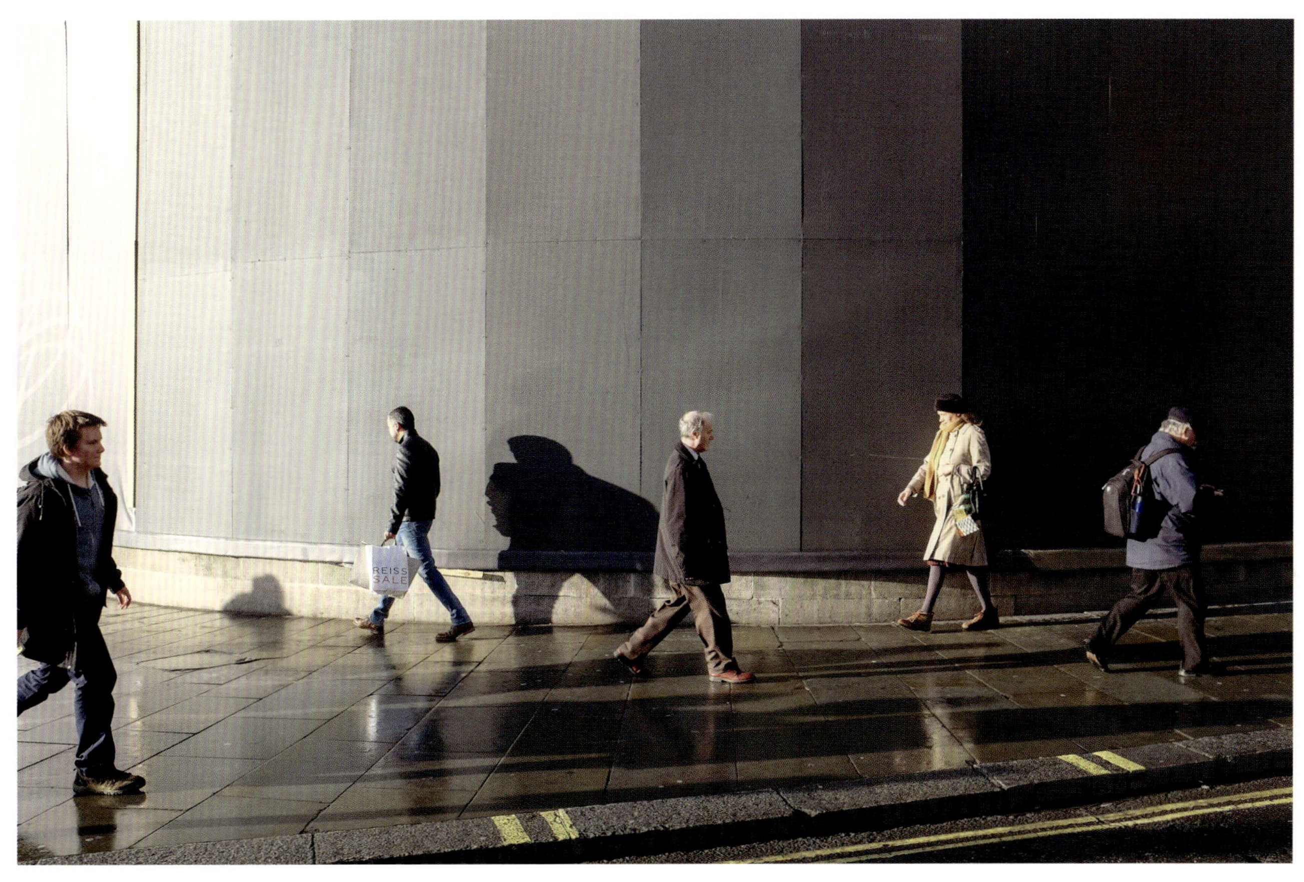
REISS
SALE

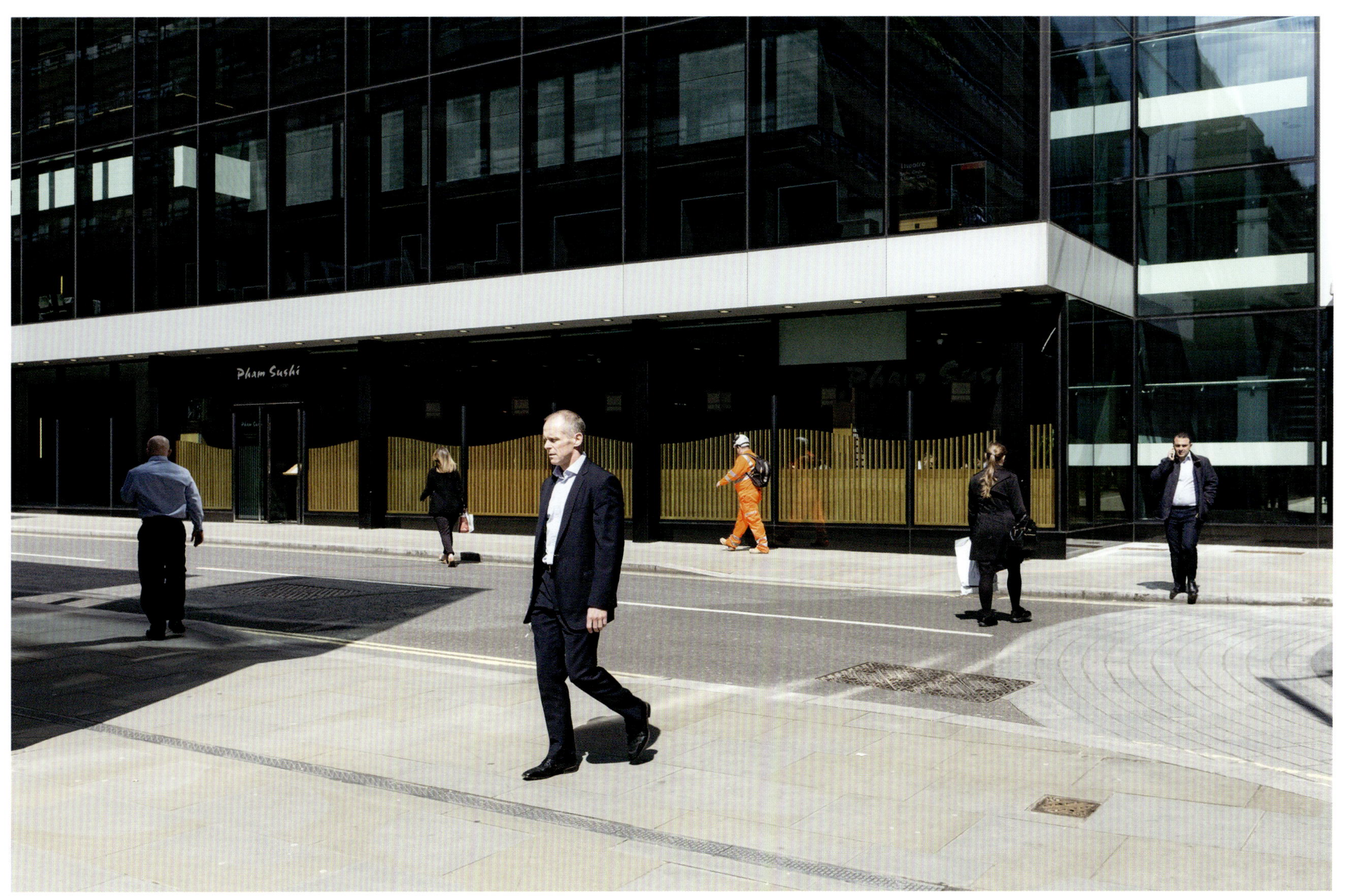
Pham Sushi

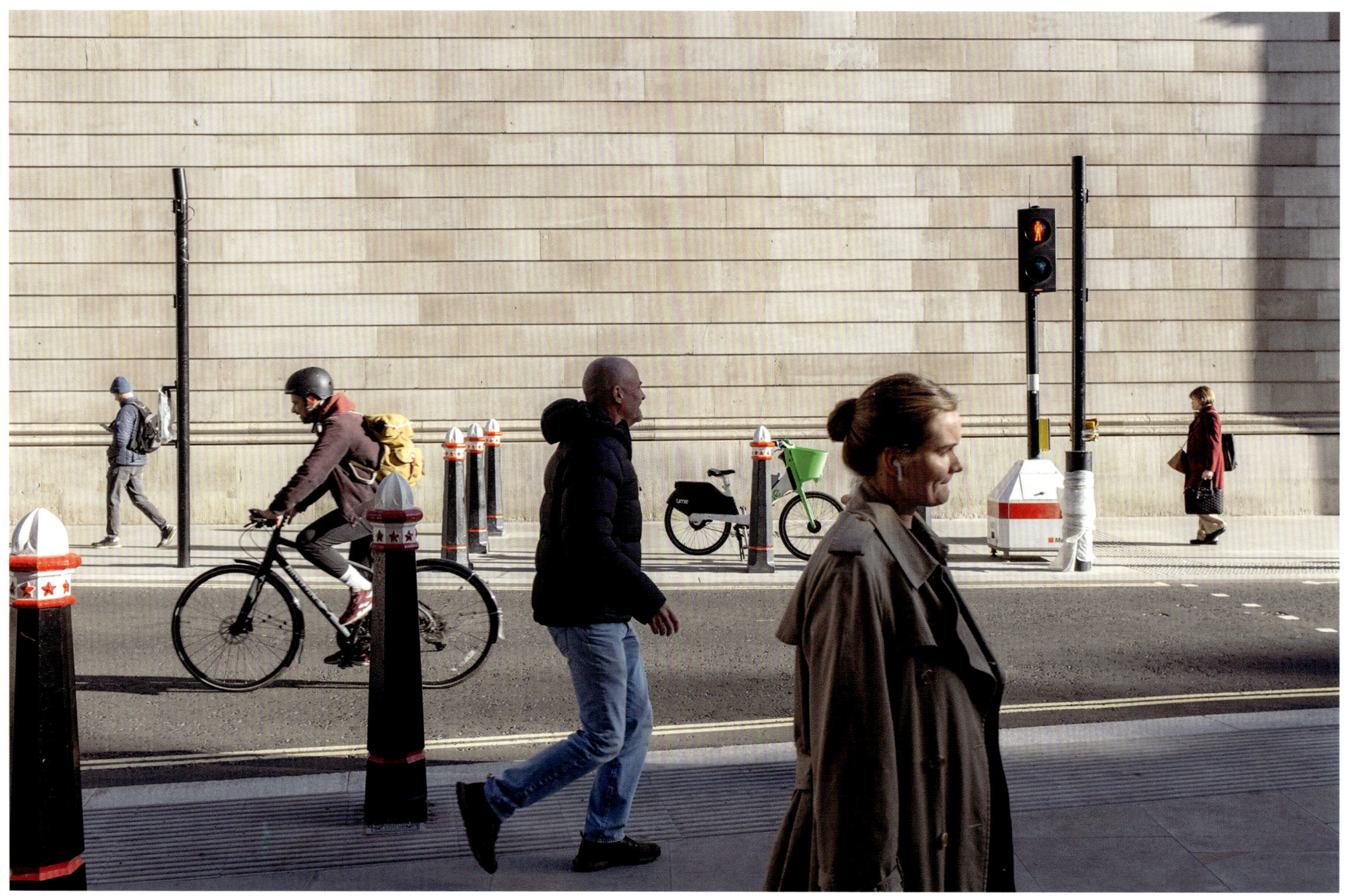

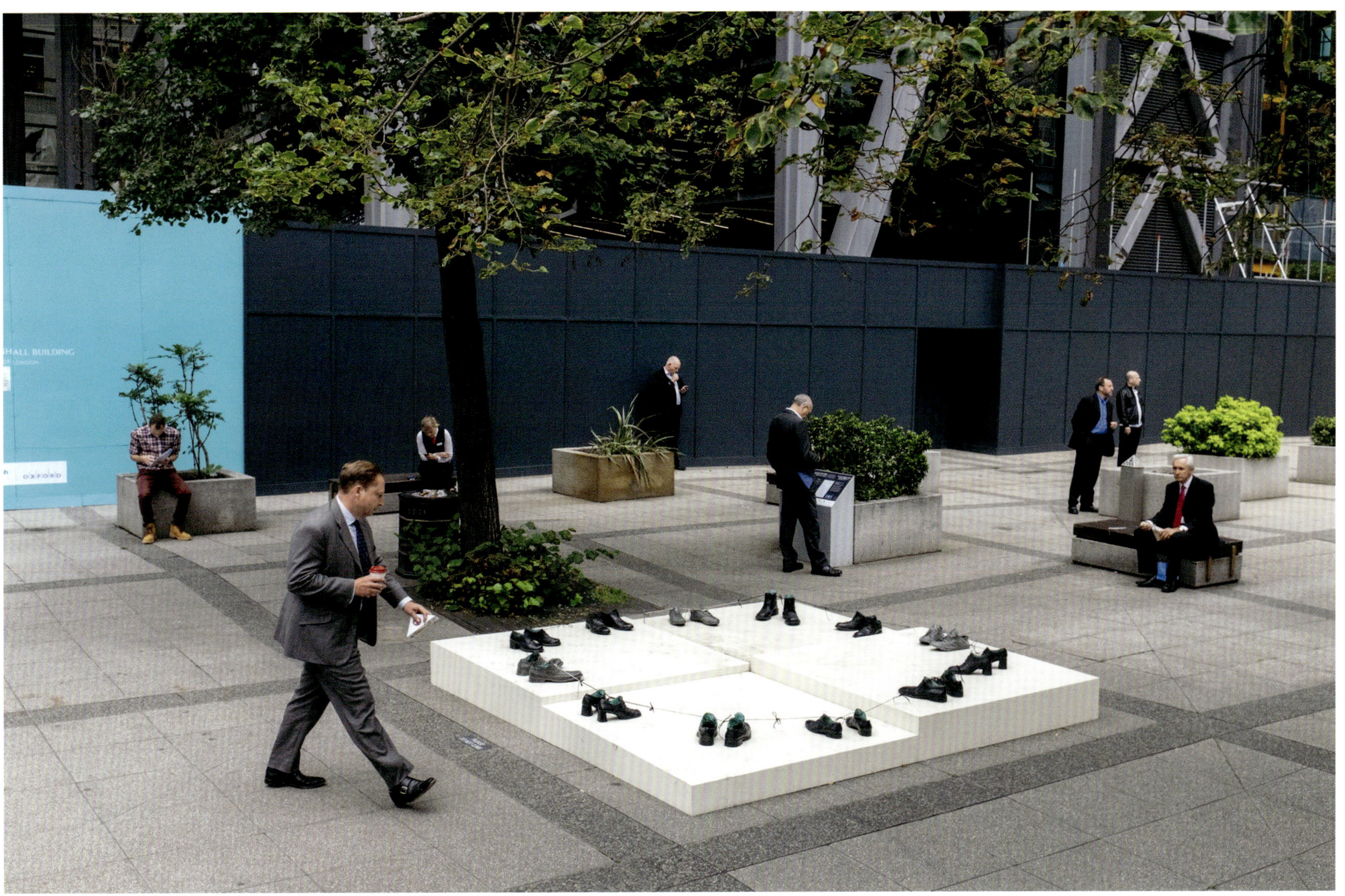
SHALL BUILDING
OXFORD

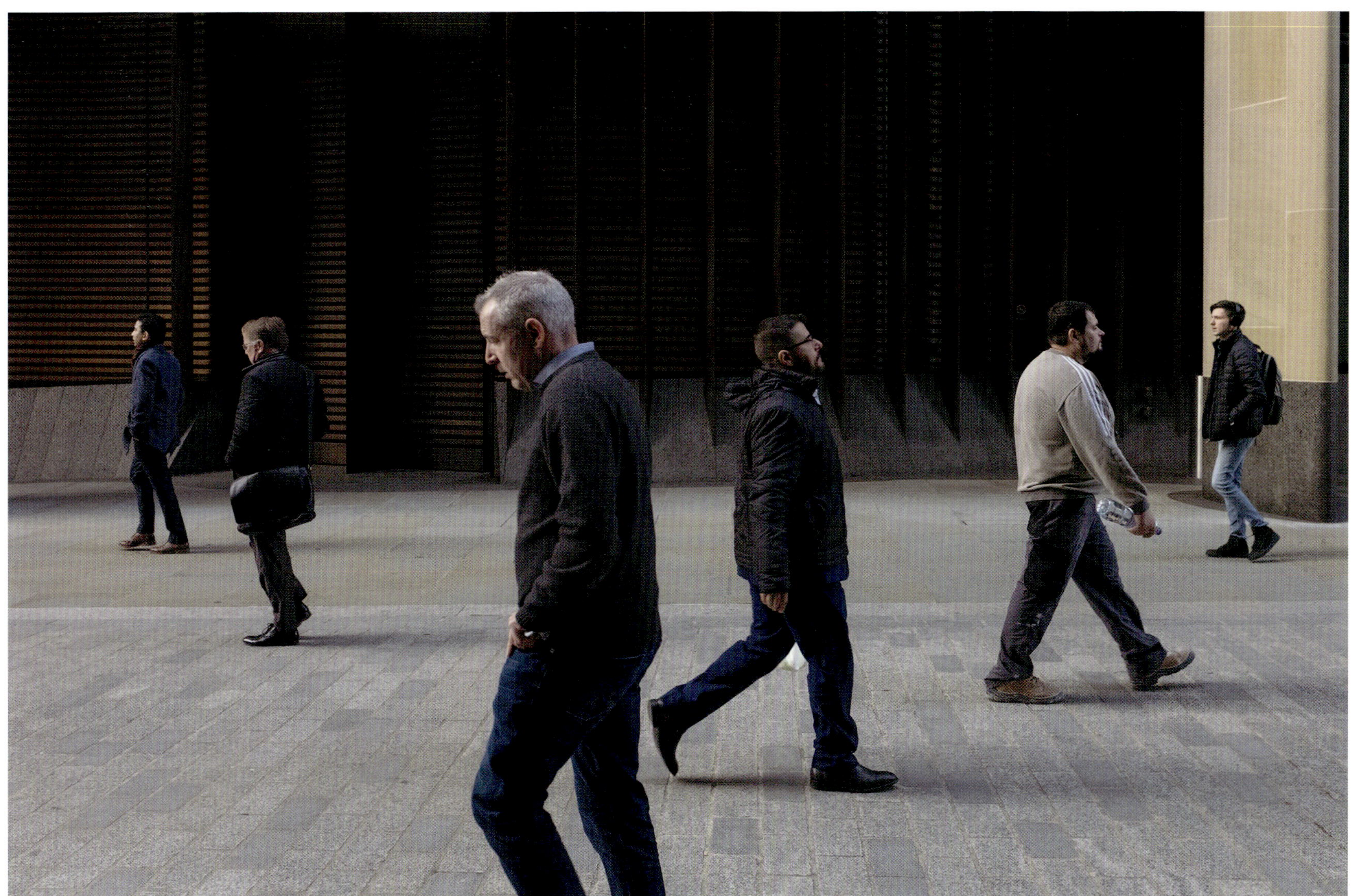

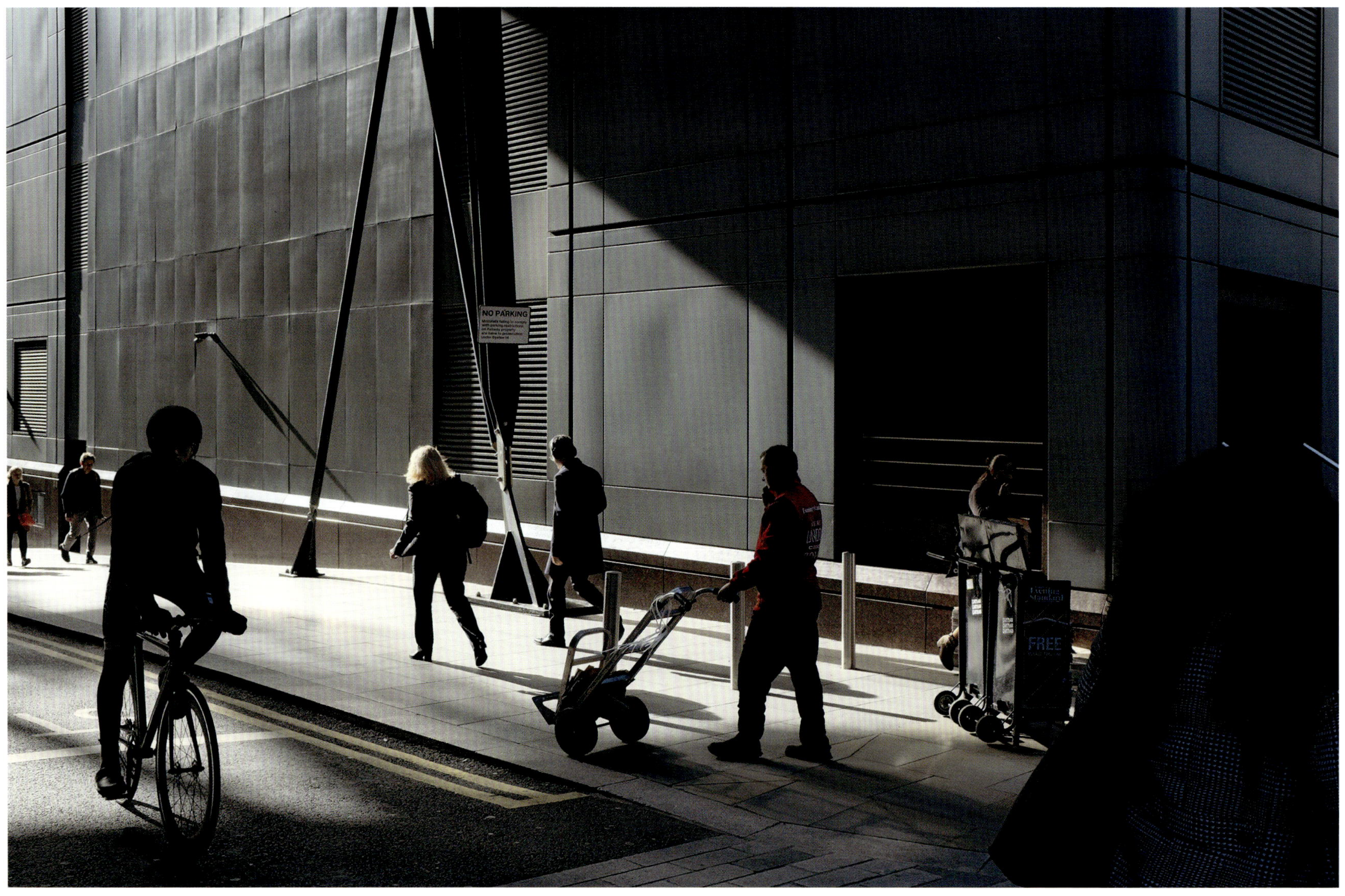
NO PARKING
FREE

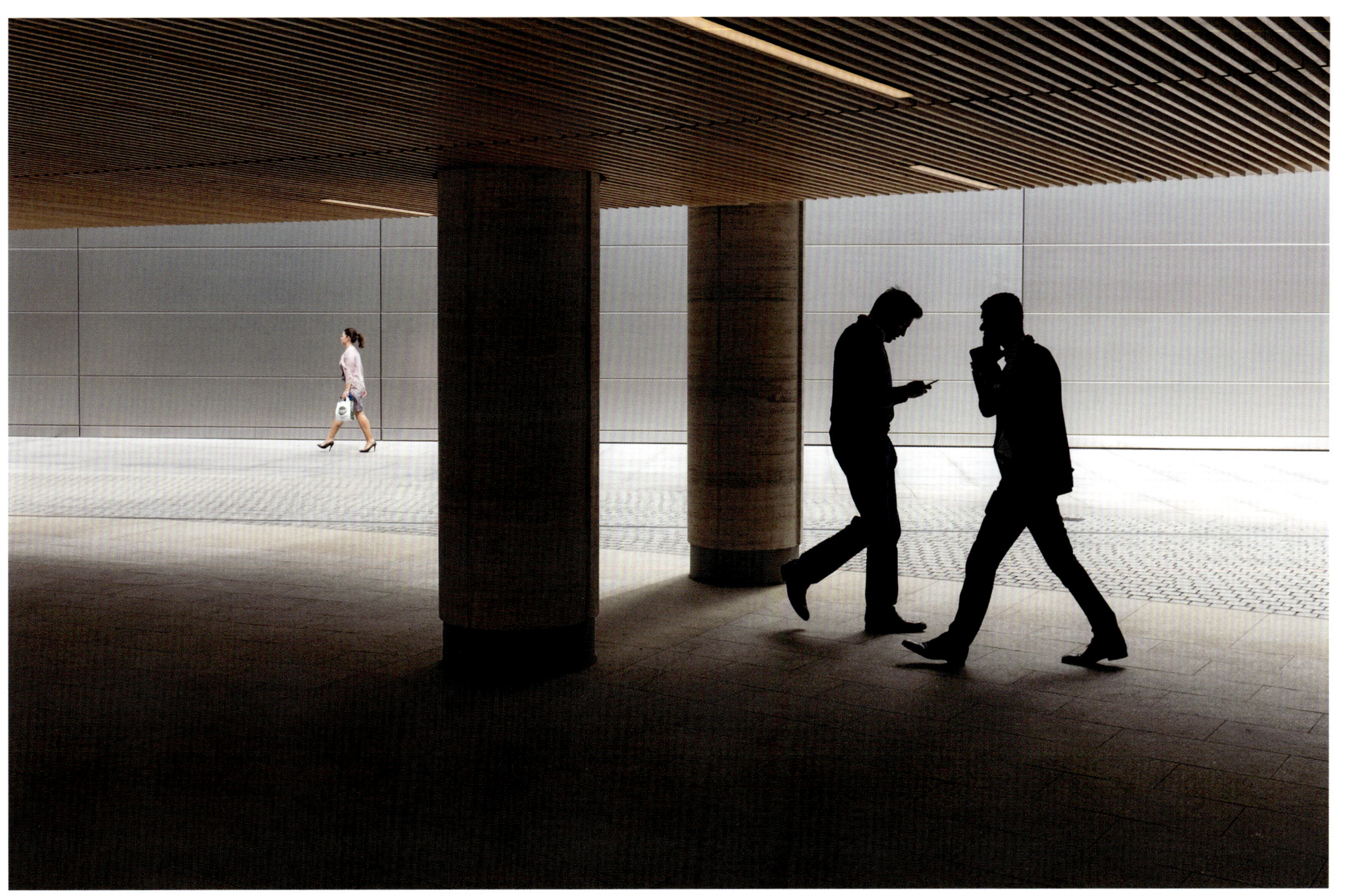

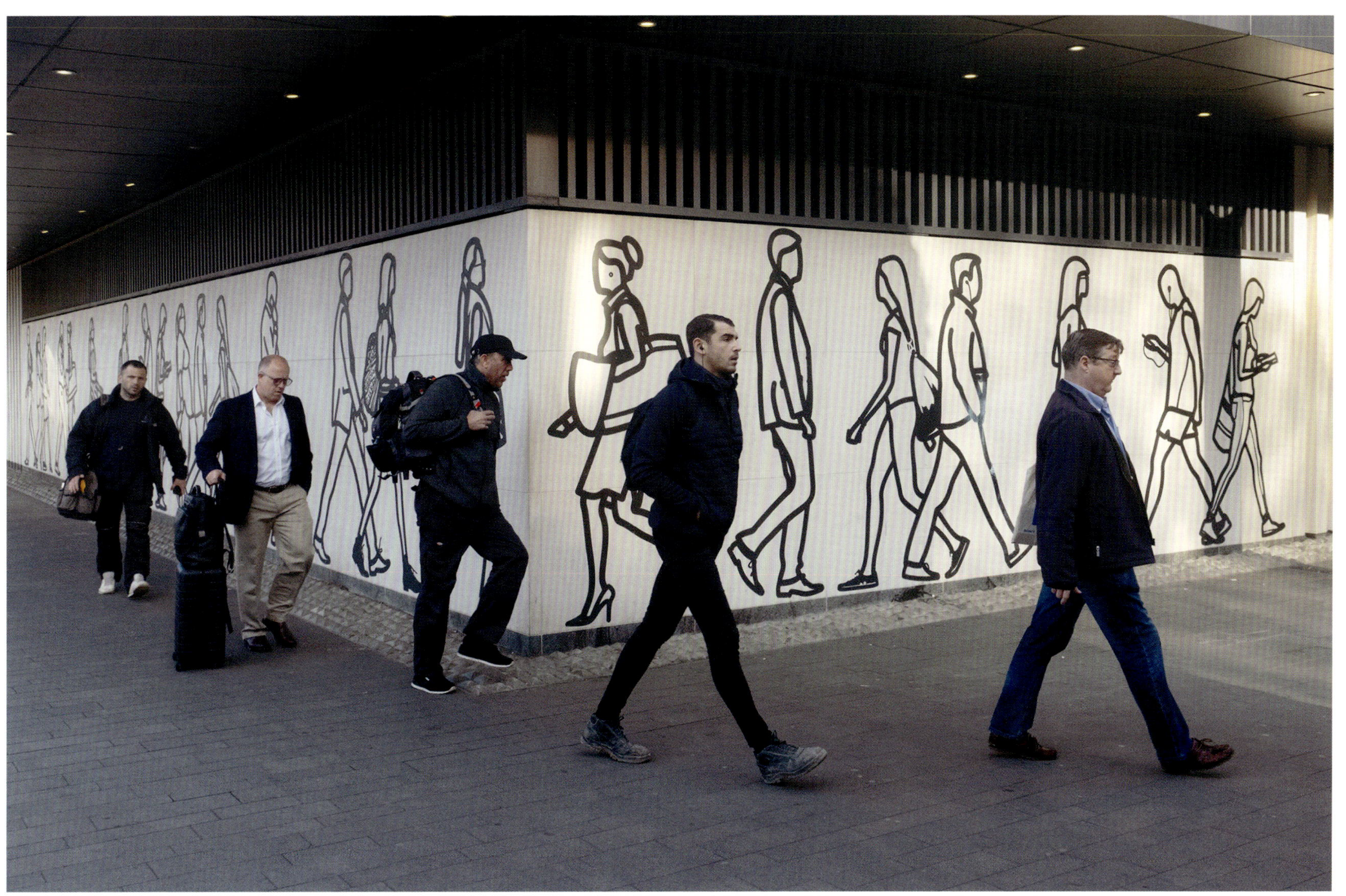

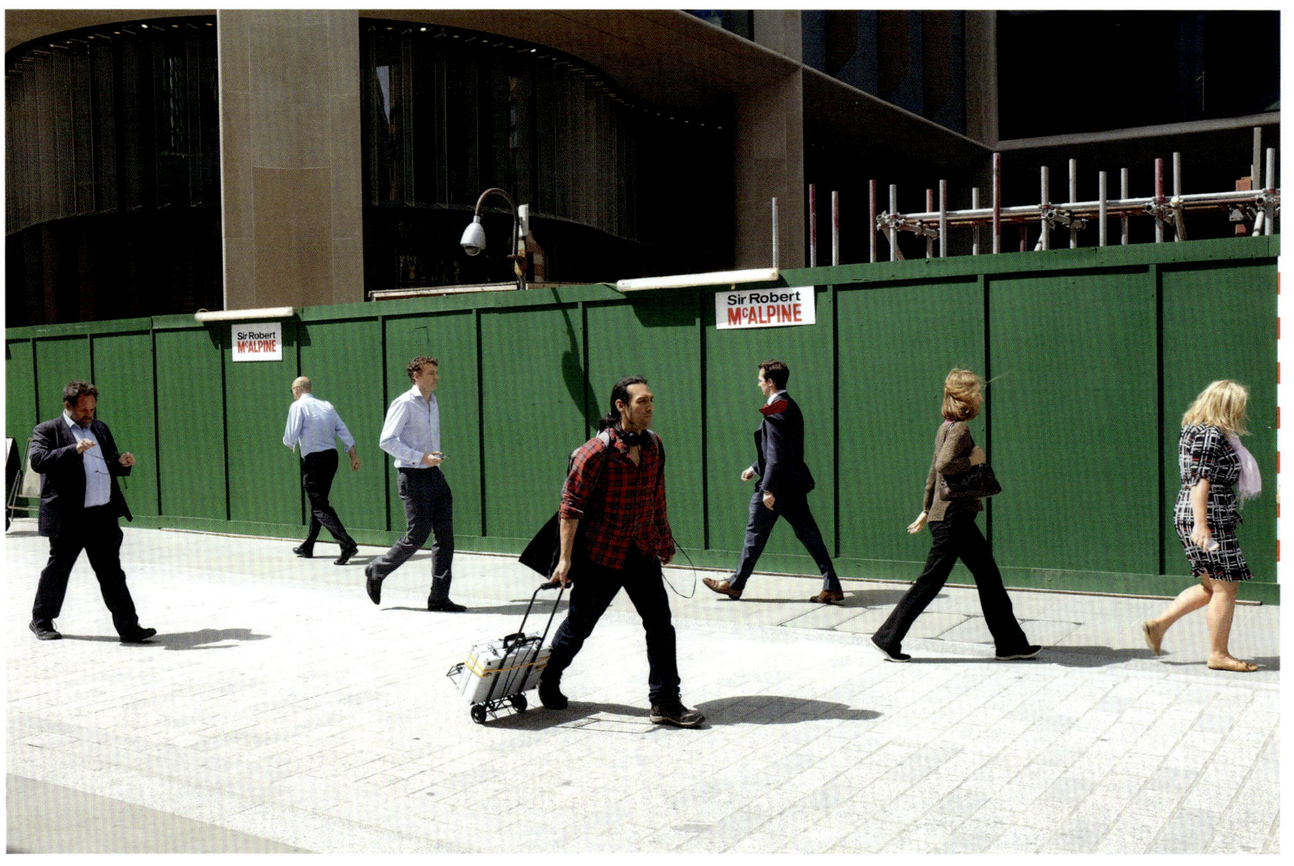
Sir Robert
McALPINE
Sir Robert
McALPINE

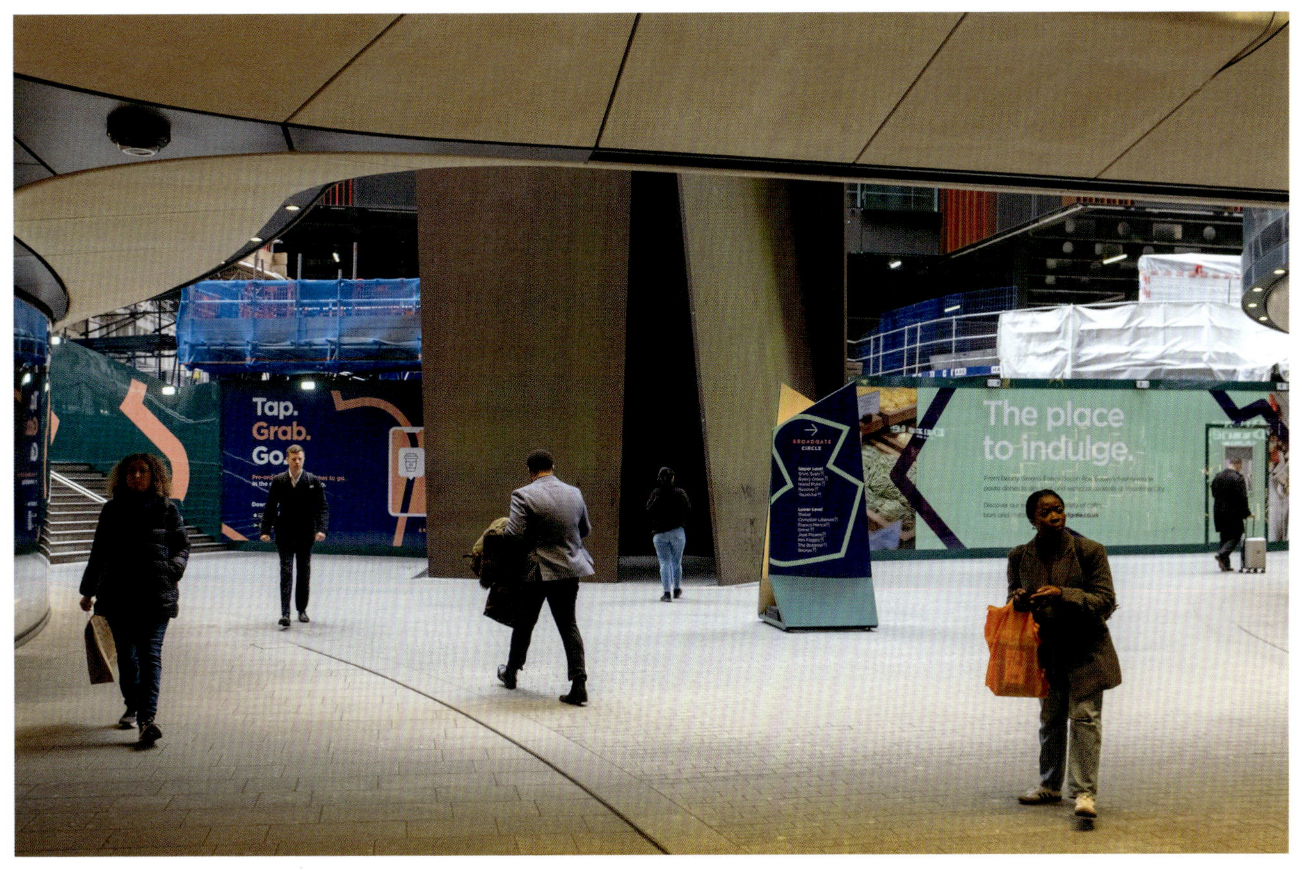
Tap.
Grab.
Go.
The place
to indulge.

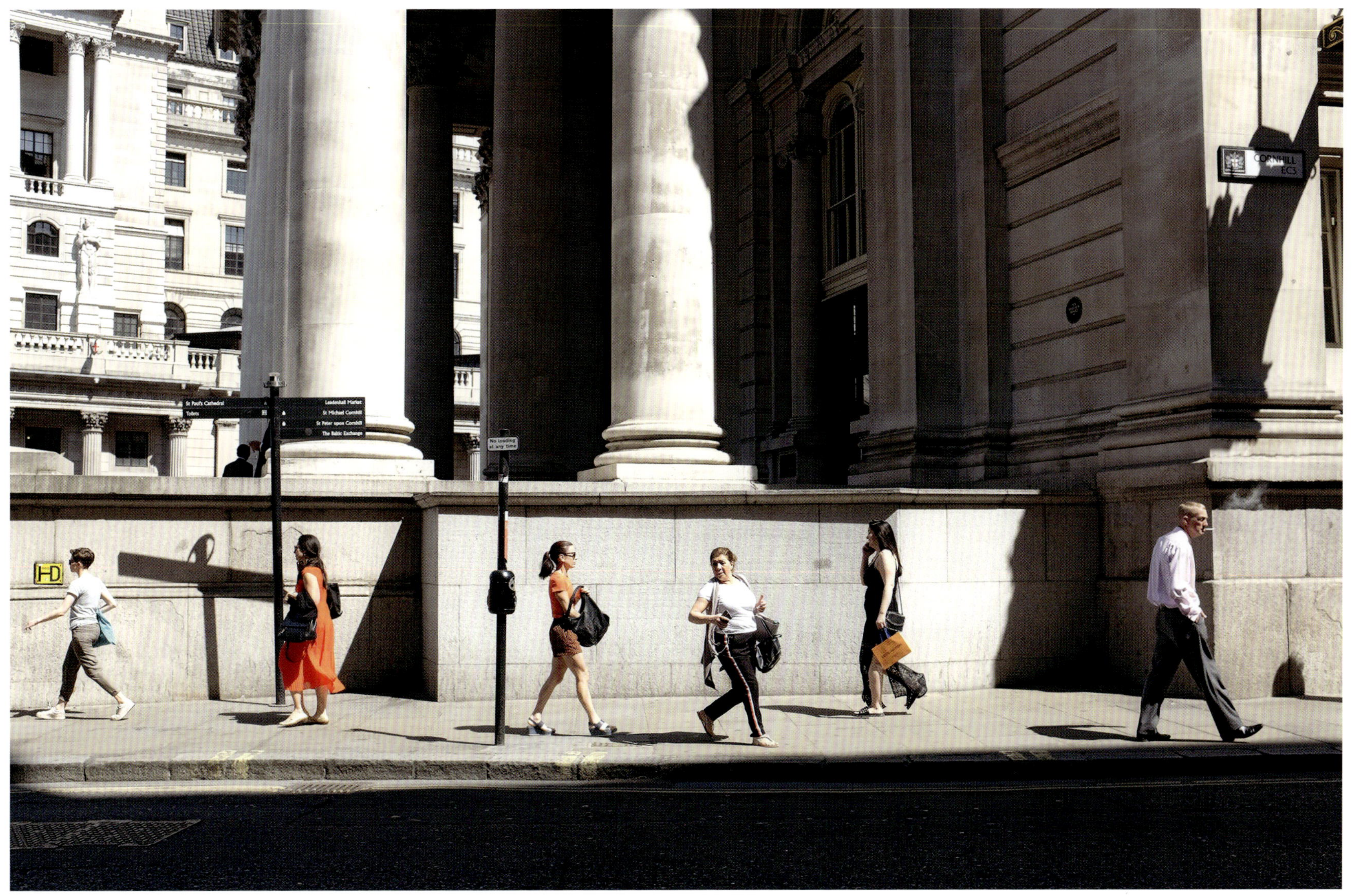
St Paul's Cathedral
Toilets
Leadenhall Market
St Michael Cornhill
St Peter upon Cornhill
The Baltic Exchange
No loading at any time
HD
CORNHILL EC3

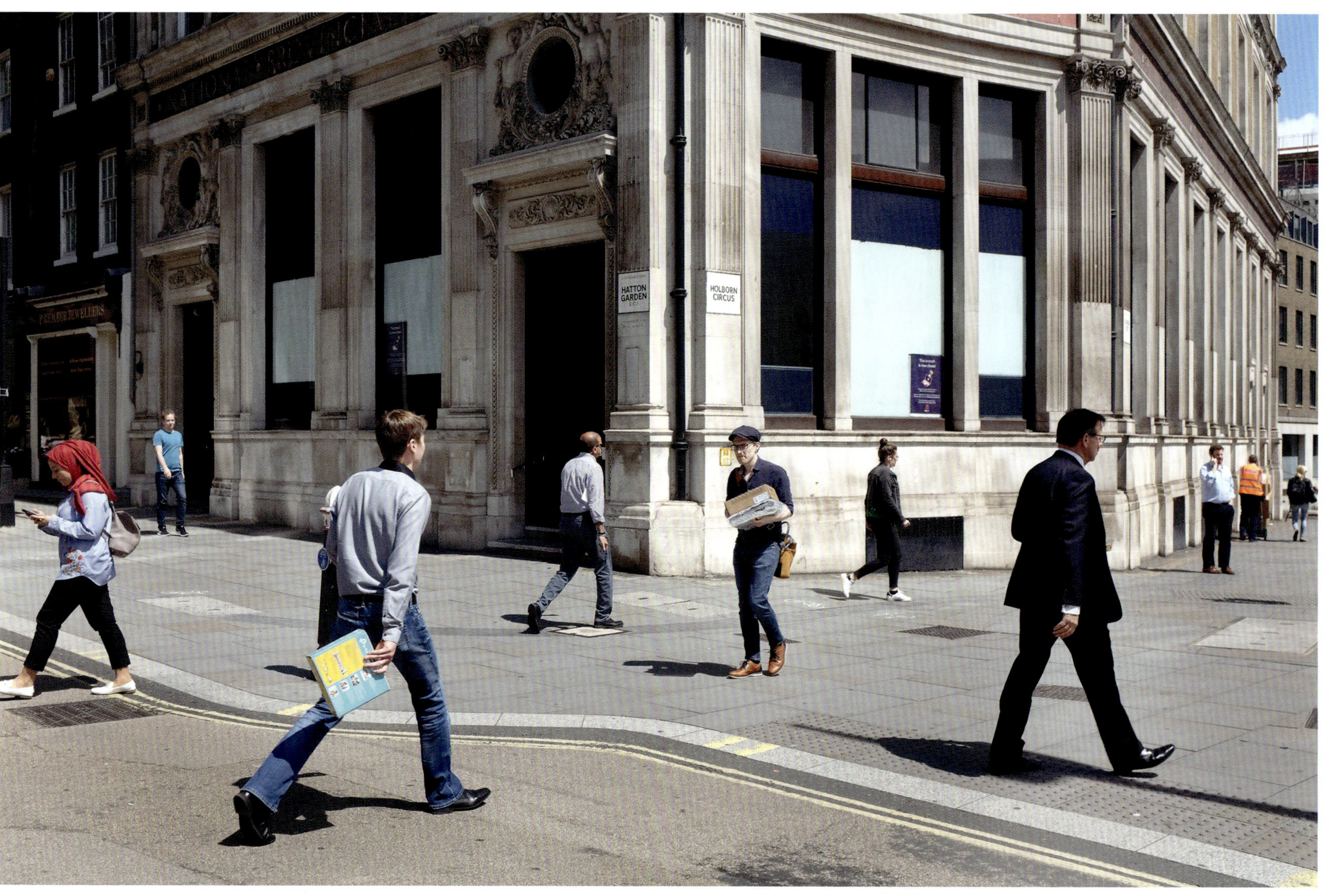
HATTON
GARDEN
HOLBORN
CIRCUS

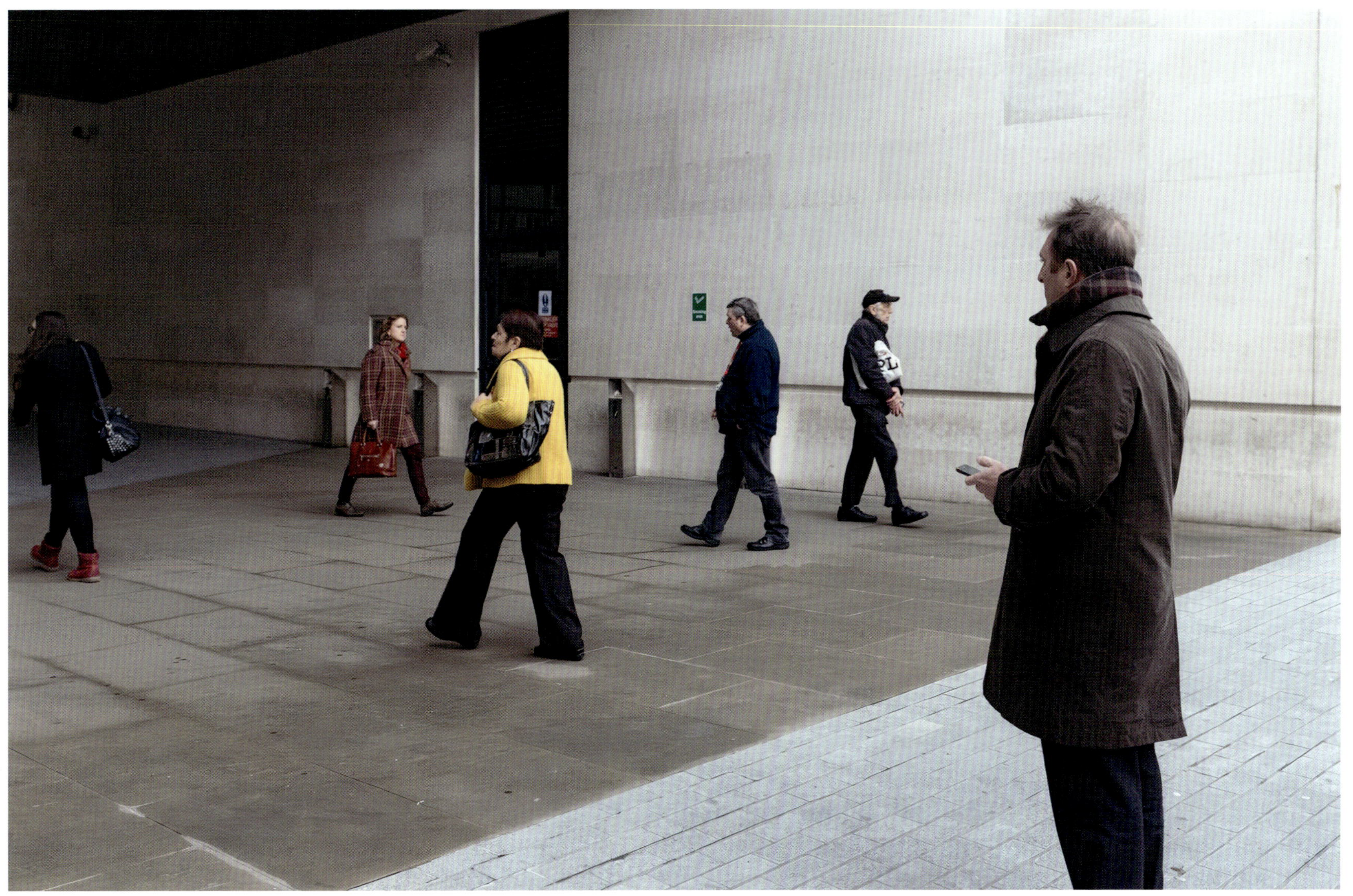

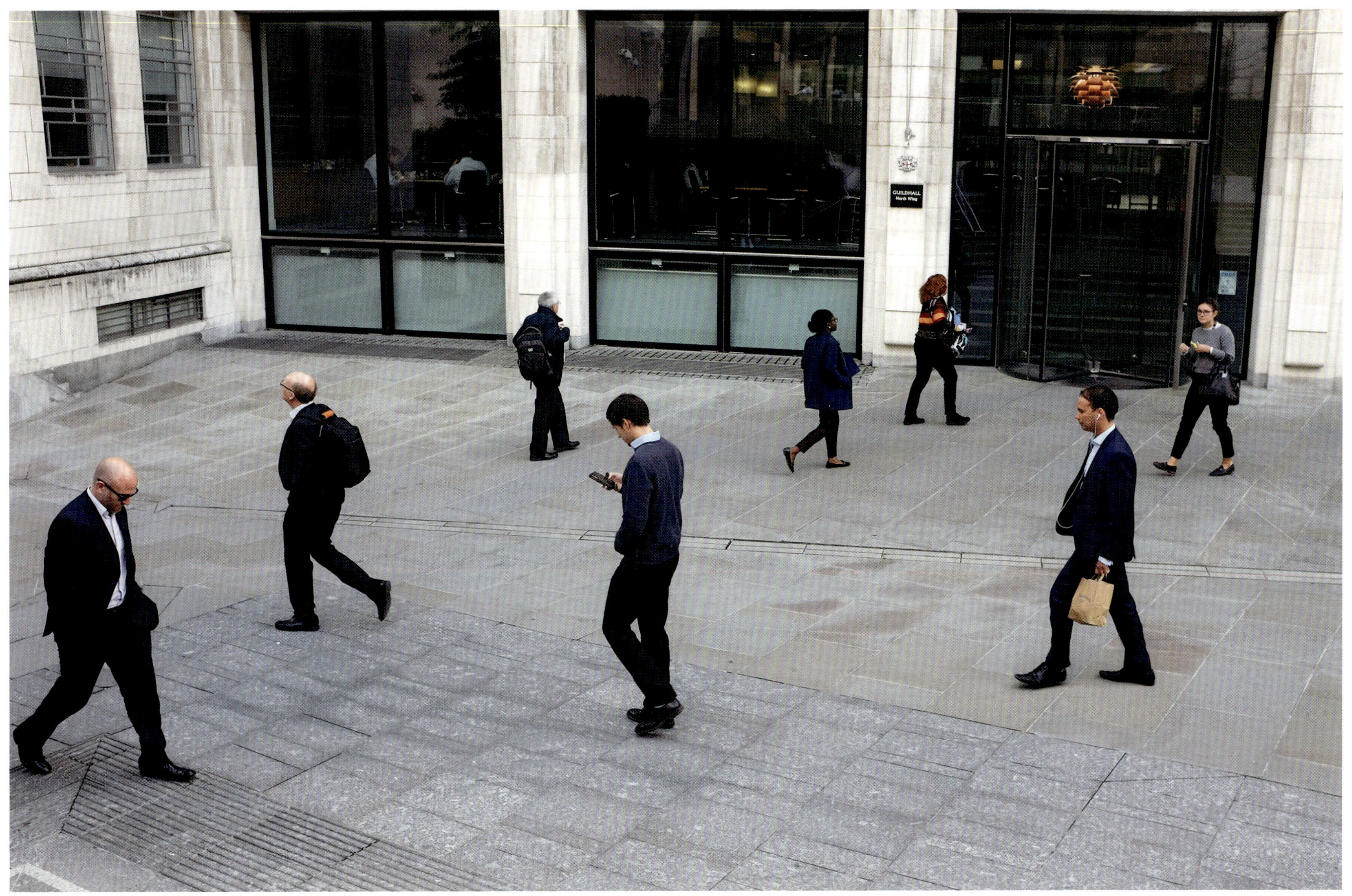
GUILDHALL
North Wing

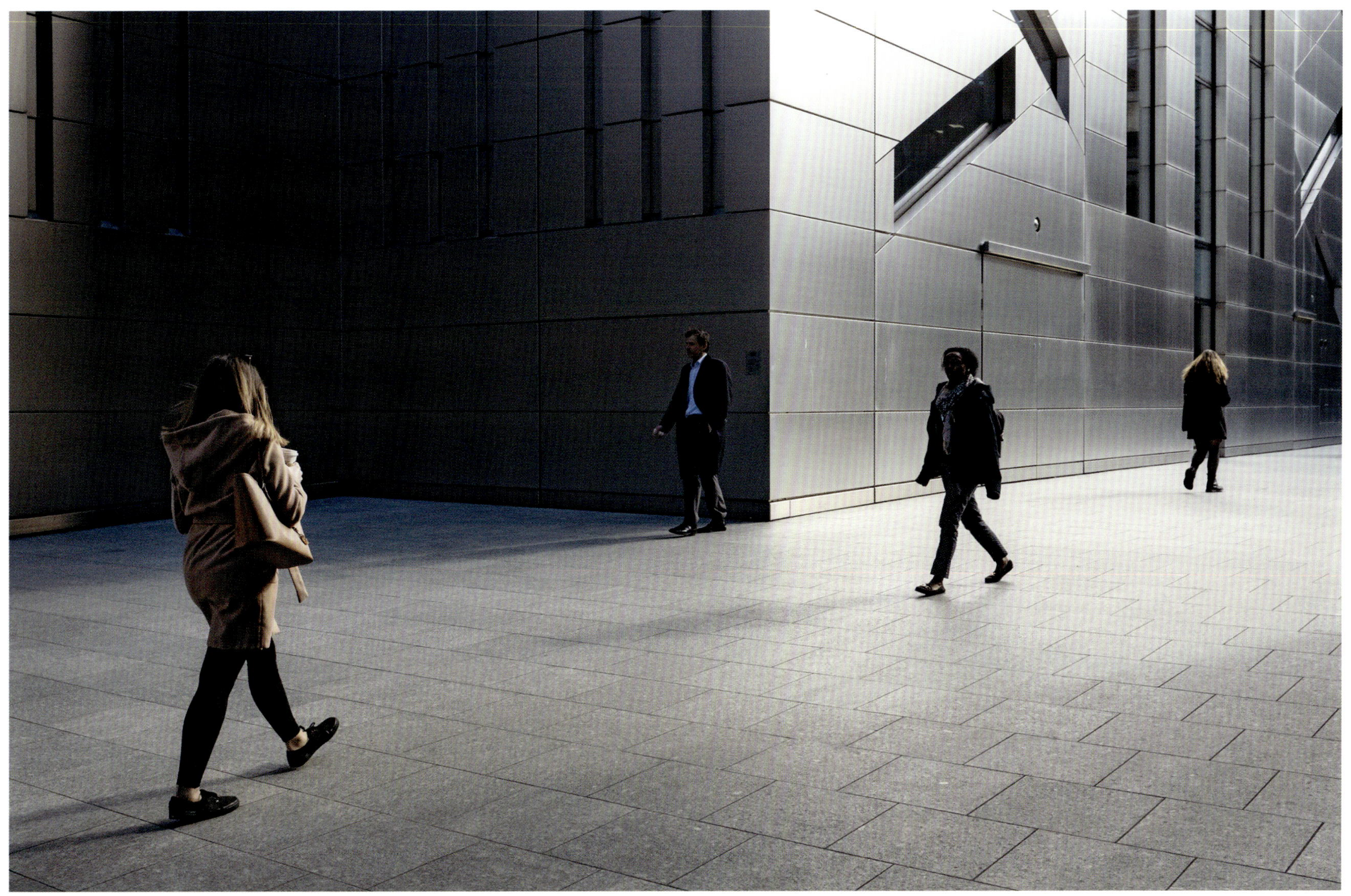

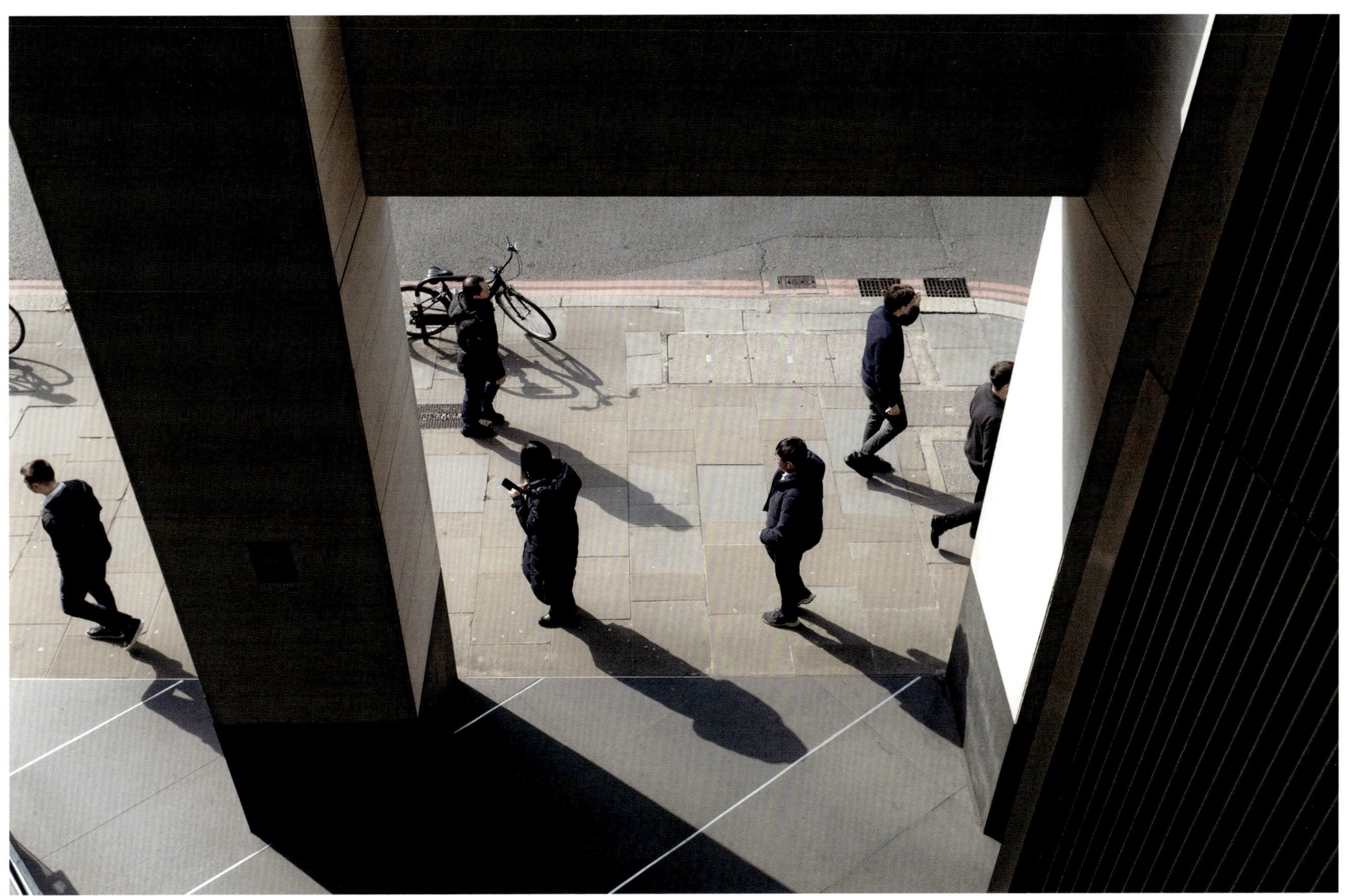

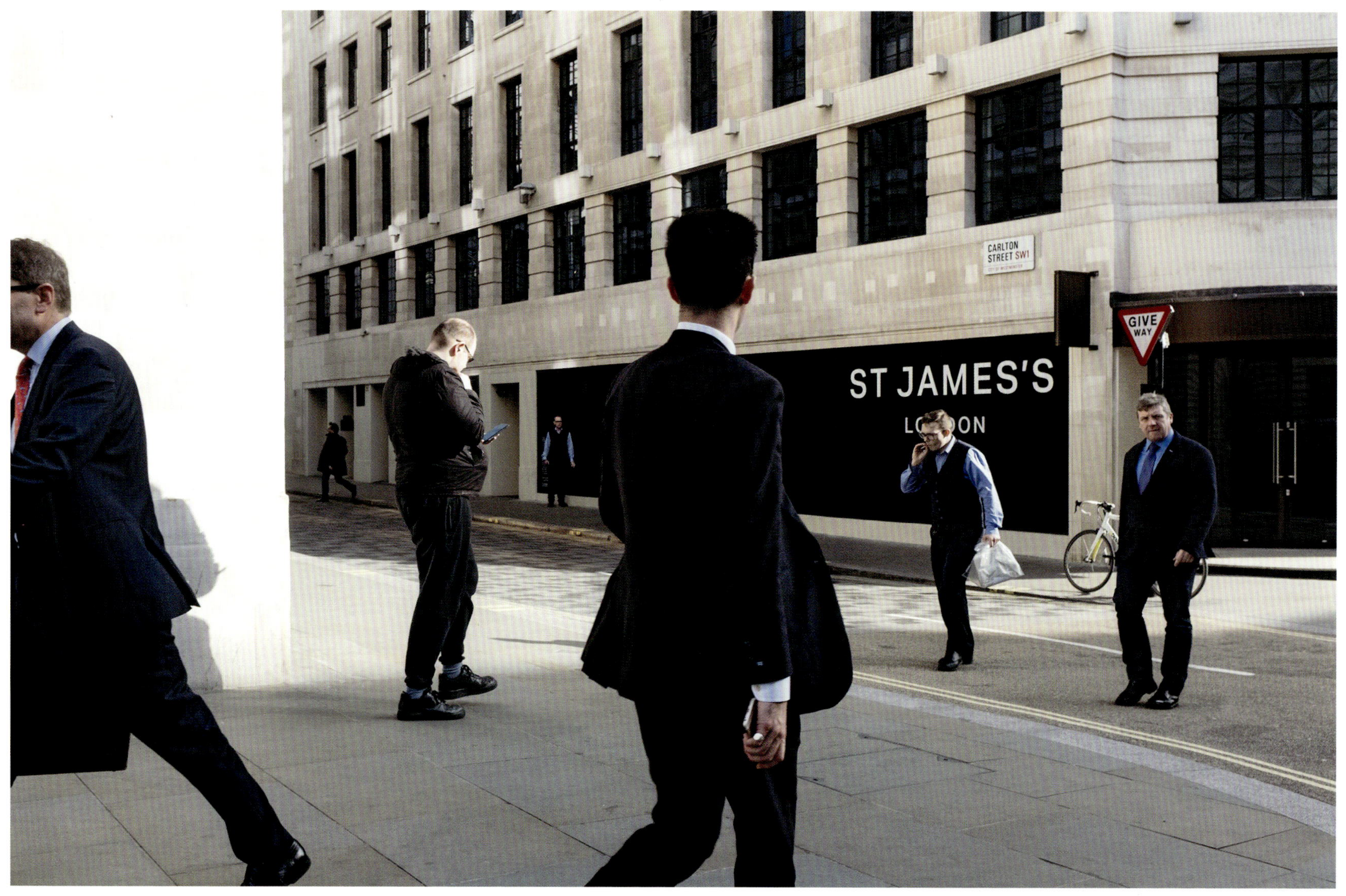
CARLTON
STREET SW1
GIVE
WAY
ST JAMES'S

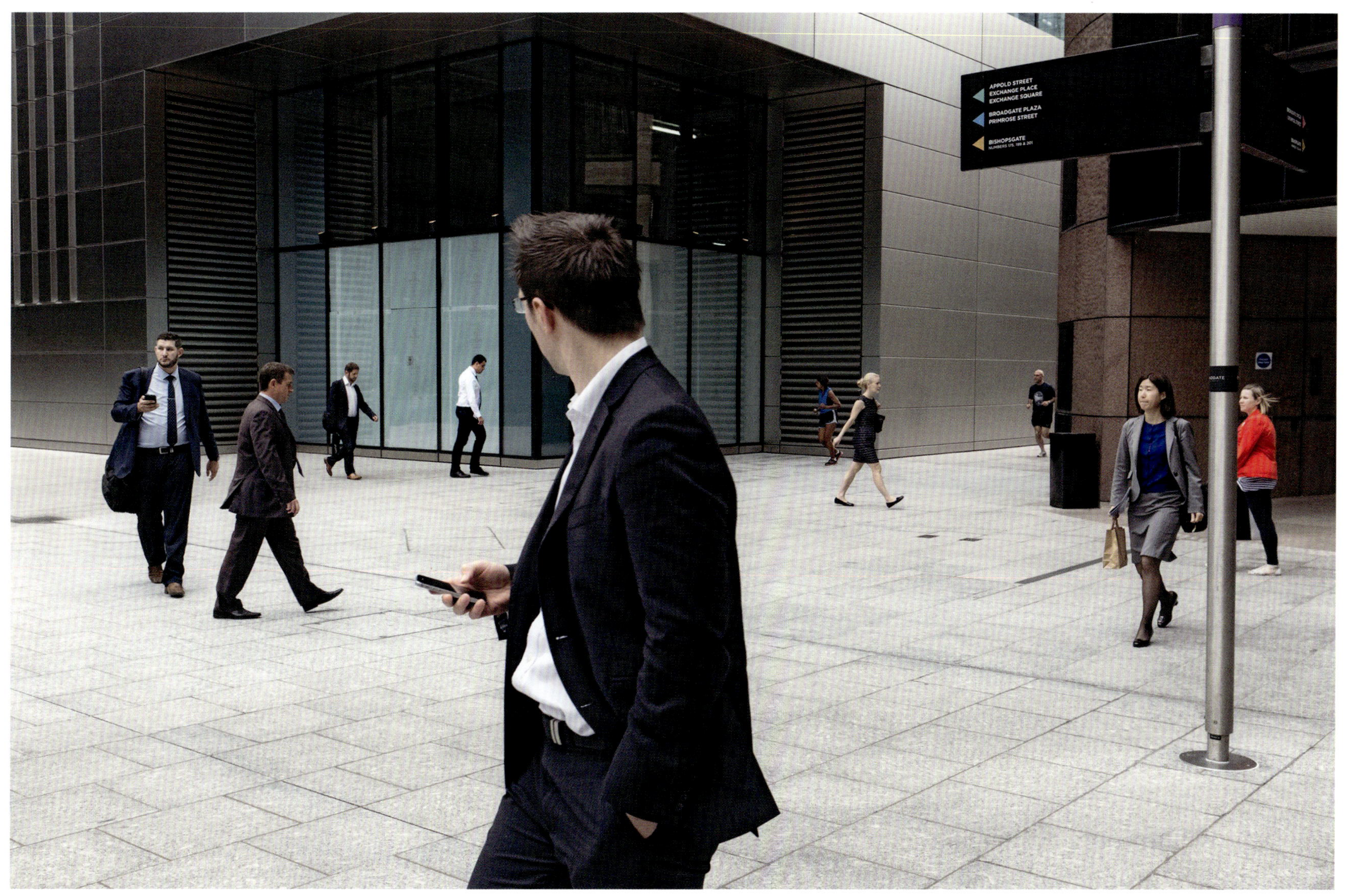
APPOLD STREET
EXCHANGE PLACE
EXCHANGE SQUARE
BROADGATE PLAZA
PRIMROSE STREET
BISHOPSGATE
NUMBERS 175, 199 & 201

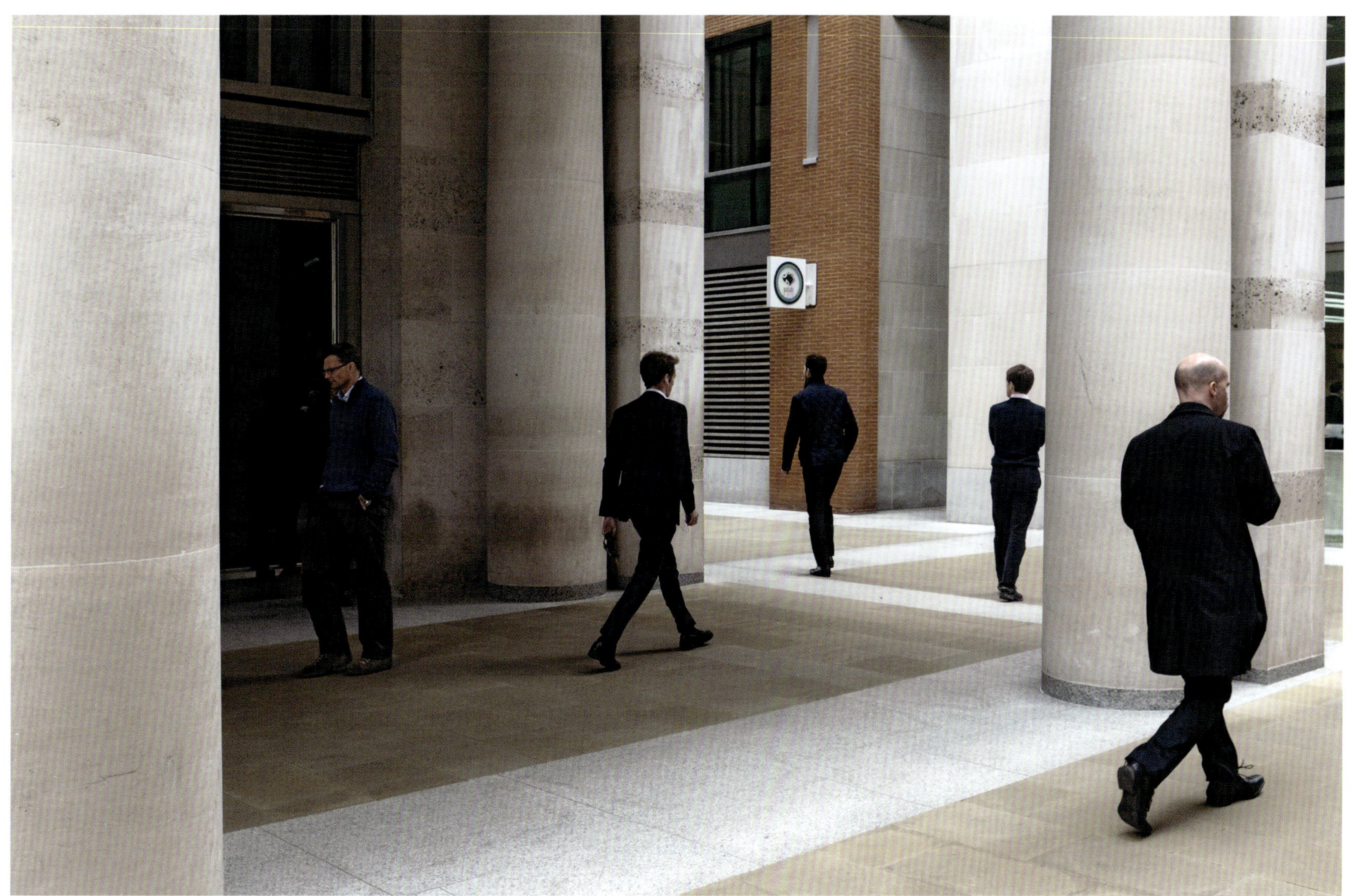

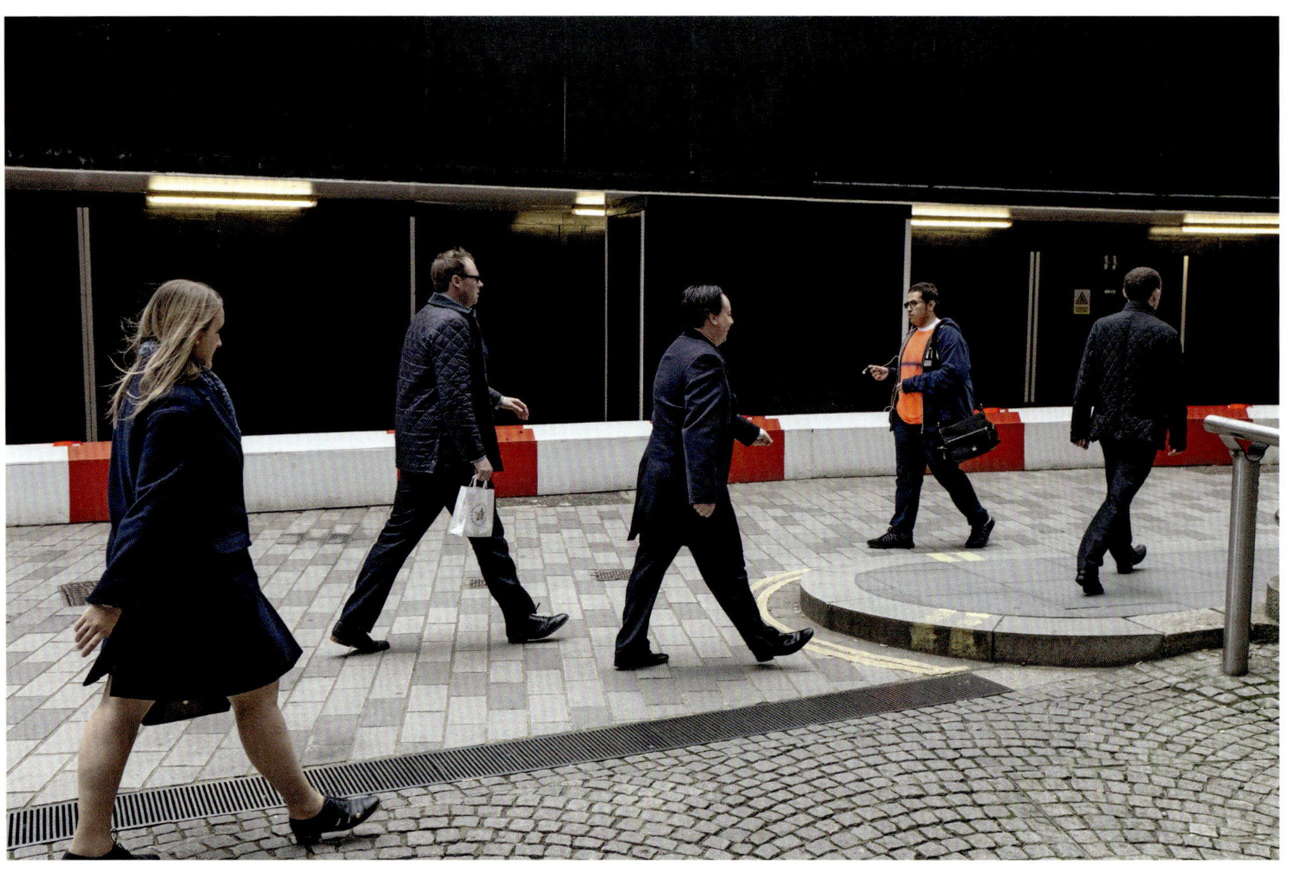

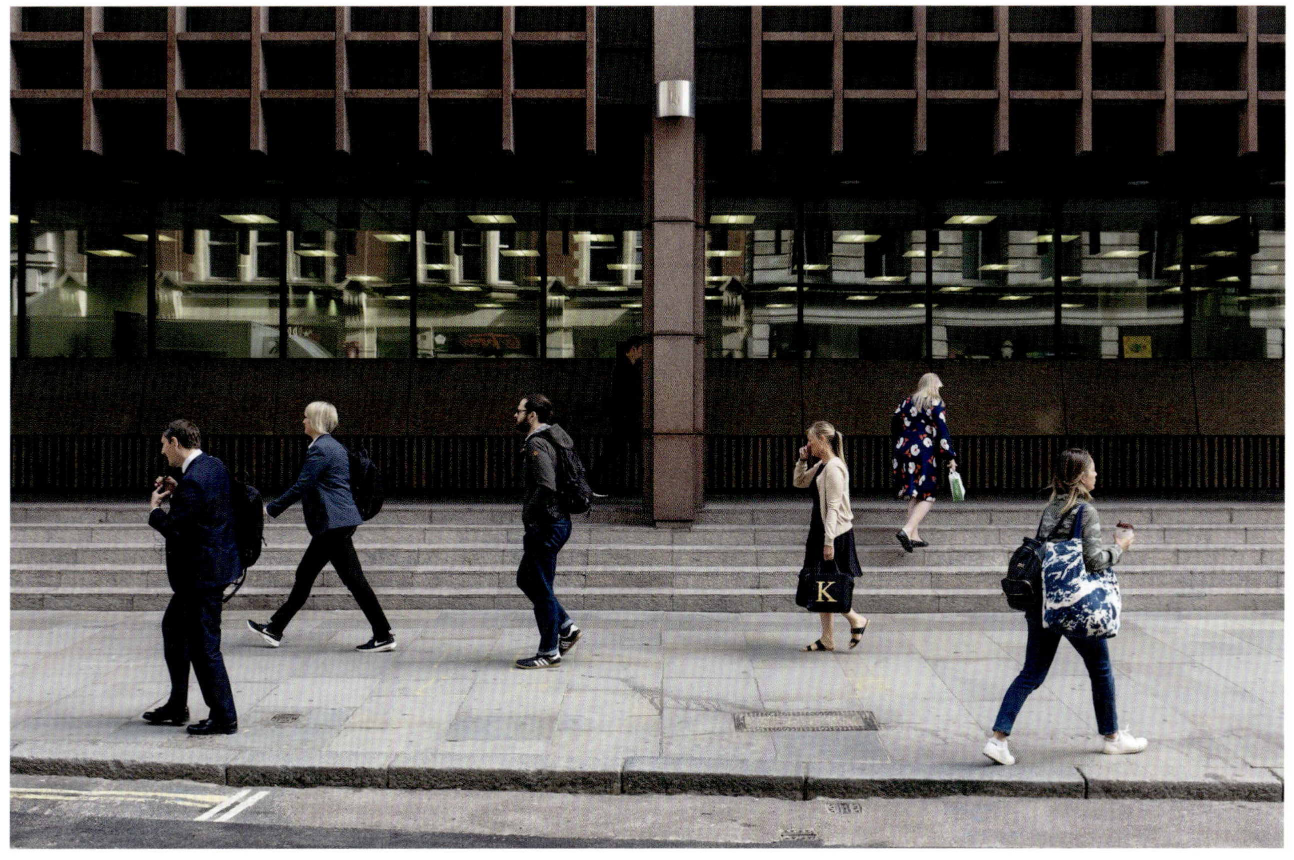
K

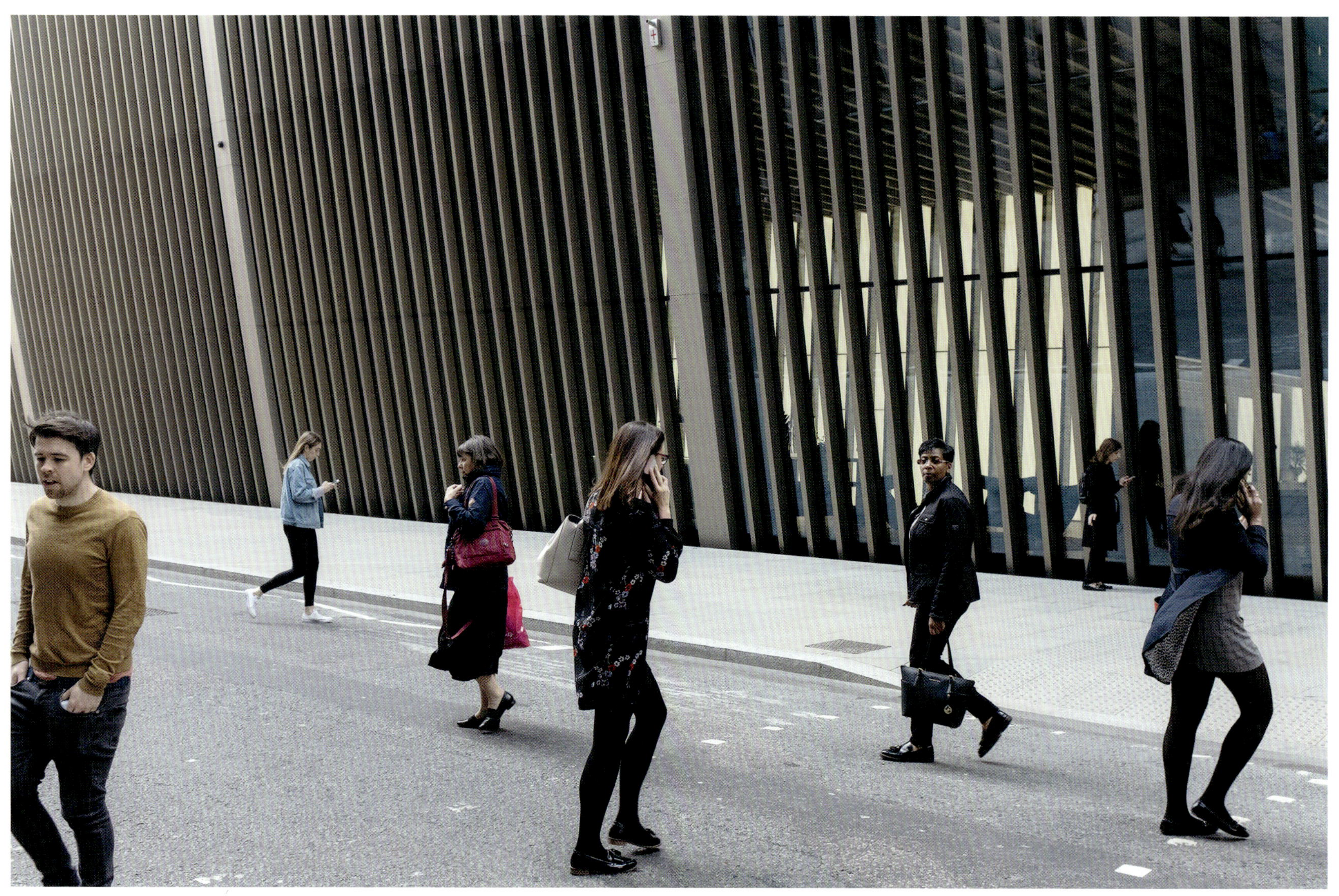

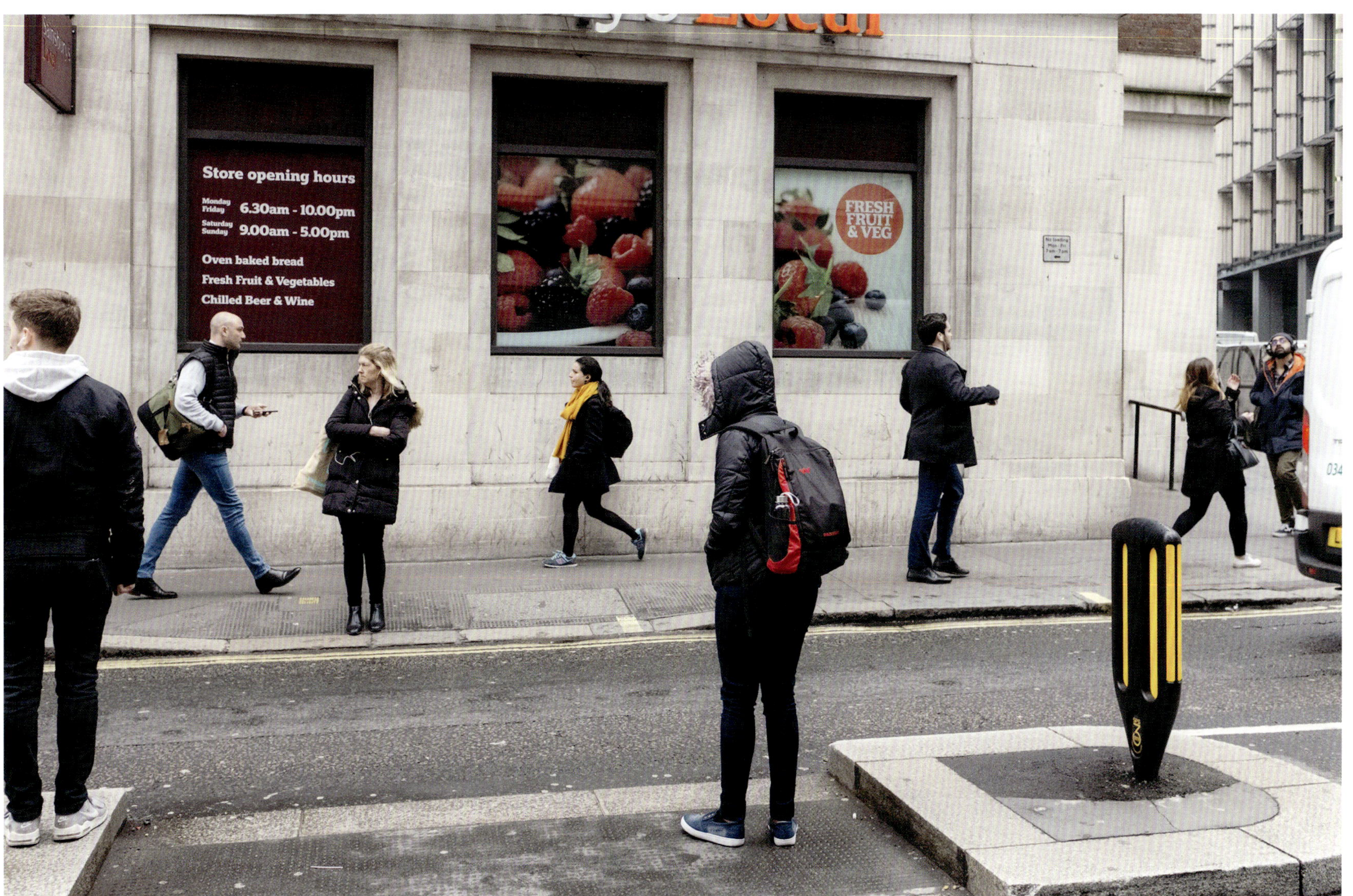
Store opening hours
Monday Friday 6.30am - 10.00pm
Saturday Sunday 9.00am - 5.00pm
Oven baked bread
Fresh Fruit & Vegetables
Chilled Beer & Wine
FRESH FRUIT & VEG

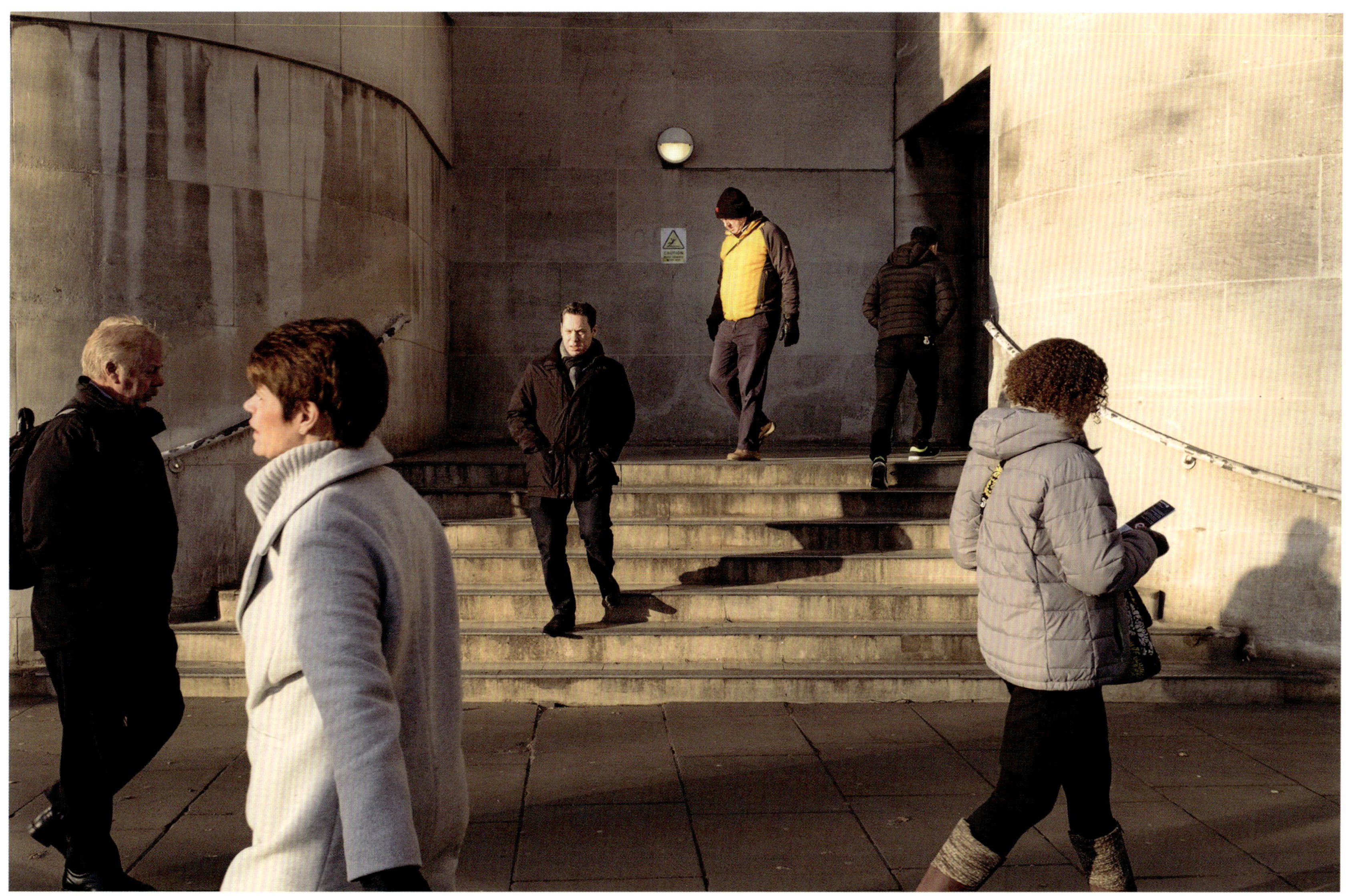

PLATELIST